THE CABIN

THE CABIN

REMINISCENCE AND DIVERSIONS

DAVID MAMET

TURTLE BAY BOOKS

A DIVISION OF RANDOM HOUSE

NEW YORK 1992

Portions of this work were originally published in the *Chicago
Tribune, Hampton's, Harper's, HG,* the *Los Angeles Times Magazine,*
and *The Traveler.*

Library of Congress Cataloging-in-Publication Data
Mamet, David.
The cabin : reminiscence and diversions / David Mamet.
p.   cm.
ISBN 0-679-41558-0
1. Mamet, David—Biography.
2. Dramatists, American—20th
century—Biography.   I. Title.
PS3563.A4345Z465   1992
812'.54—dc20
[B]   92-58324

Manufactured in the United States of America
24689753

FOR MY SISTER, LYNN

ACKNOWLEDGMENTS

I would like to thank Joni Evans and Julie Grau for their interest in and care of these essays; and I would like to thank my assistant, Harriet Voyt, for her lovely good nature and for her help with the preparation of this book.

PROLOGUE:

RUTLAND GATE

I met Pat Buckley on my first trip to London. I had just turned thirty, and he was something over eighty.

We were walking near Parliament, and he gestured and said that his solicitors' offices were just nearby. I was shopping for a lawyer myself, and I asked him how long the folks over there had been his solicitors. "For about a hundred twenty years," he said.

He remembered, as a child, he said, being taken to see Queen Victoria. He had been at school with Lord Mountbatten; he was a man-about-town in the twenties. When the BBC did a retrospective on the Charleston in the seventies, Pat was remembered as a leading exponent of the dance, and he spoke about it and twenties London over the radio.

He had been in MI5 during the Second World War. He told this story: an MI5 officer friend of his had been traveling from London to Scotland by rail. The man was in a private compartment with his batman, when an enlisted man entered and said that there was another officer in the coach who somehow looked out of place. The MI5 man asked for the officer to be brought to his compartment, and he was.

The officer's papers were all in order, and there was nothing out of place about him, and nothing to excite suspicion. Nonetheless the man did not seem quite right.

"Take off your jacket," the MI5 man asked, and the officer did so. He was then asked to take off his shirt and then his undershirt, under which were seen large red welts of the sort caused by a parachute harness. The man turned out to be a German spy who had parachuted into England that morning. He was tried and executed—"lovely story," Pat said, "I could have dined out on it all throughout the War, but, of course, while the War was on, I couldn't tell it."

I think he was himself the MI5 officer on the train.

I wonder what he did during the First World War, in which he must certainly have fought, but about which he would not speak.

I know that in the late twenties and thirties he wrote travel books, which were a favorite of Queen Mary—he showed me correspondence and a photograph she had autographed to him. He also toured America in that period, lecturing about Great Britain, and was a great success, it seems. He had several quite intimately inscribed photos of a very well-known film actress on his mantel.

We walked through Knightsbridge. He took me to a decorator's shop to show me some material. There was a very pretty young woman proprietor, and she treated him with great deference, and referred to him as Major Buckley.

We stopped at a storefront tailor where he was having his suits recut. They were of excellent manufacture, and quite old, and, as he was losing weight, he was having them made over from single- to double-breasted cut.

And at the tailor he showed me an innovation of which he was proud: he'd had the man sew a two-inch-diameter red felt circle over the label on the inside of the collar of his raincoat. Everyone in London had the same coat, he told me, and this made it a breeze to reclaim his from the coat-check room.

This seemed to me a terrific idea, and for years I have been meaning, and still mean, to do it to my coats.

We went back to his flat in Rutland Gate and he told me this:

A friend of a niece of his had come to visit London from the States. She came round to his flat, he made her some lunch, and, when she had left, he noticed that his wristwatch, which he had left on his dresser, was missing. He told me it was a Patek Philippe watch in platinum, that he had worn it for over fifty years, and that she had certainly taken it.

On my next trip to London five years later, Pat told me the story of the watch again, as if the theft had happened to him just the day before.

I was reading a posh British magazine the other day, and came across a real estate listing for a beautiful flat in Rutland Gate. It had several photos of the flat and listed the amenities, and, having visited there myself, I agreed with the description. One of the photos showed the mantel, and, on it, the photo of the very famous film star.

Well, we have no more Victorian gentlemen with us.

I would have liked to have known more about MI5, and the Great War, and his affair with the film star.

I would have liked to have listened to him tell about the film community in the thirties, and whether it was in fact he who caught the German spy.

He was a gracious man, and good to talk to me. It occurs to me that he must have, consciously or not, told me the story of the Patek watch because he was worried that I might take something from him. I'd like to put another coloration on it, but if the reminiscence is going to have any worth it should, I think, be accurate.

This volume is, mainly, travel and reminiscence, and, if I am going to analyze the content accurately, I suppose it must mean that I, too, am getting old.

Best wishes,

David Mamet

CONTENTS

THE CABIN

THE RAKE

There was the incident of the rake and there was the incident of the school play, and it seems to me that they both took place at the round kitchen table.

The table was not in the kitchen proper, but in an area called the "nook," which held its claim to that small measure of charm by dint of a waist-high wall separating it from an adjacent area known as the living room.

All family meals were eaten in the nook. There was a dining room to the right, but, as in most rooms of that name at that time and in those surroundings, it was never used.

The round table was of wrought iron and topped with glass; it was noteworthy for that glass, for it was more than once and rather more than several times, I am inclined to think, that my stepfather would grow so angry as to bring some object down on the glass top, shattering it, thus giving us to know how we had forced him out of control.

And it seems that most times when he would shatter the table, as often as that might have been, he would cut some portion of himself on the glass, or that he or his wife, our mother, would cut their hands picking up the glass afterward, and that we children were to understand, and did understand, that these wounds were our fault.

So the table was associated in our minds with the notion of blood.

The house was in a brand-new housing development in the southern suburbs. The new community was built upon, and now bordered, the remains of what had once been a cornfield. When our new family moved in, there were but a few homes in the development completed, and a few more under construction. Most streets were mud, and boasted a house here or there, and many empty lots marked out by white stakes.

The house we lived in was the development's model home. The first time we had seen it, it had signs plastered on the front and throughout the interior telling of the various conveniences it contained. And it had a lawn, one of the only homes in the new community that did.

My stepfather was fond of the lawn, and he detailed me and my sister to care for it, and one fall afternoon we found ourselves assigned to rake the leaves.

Why this chore should have been so hated I cannot say, except that we children, and I especially, felt ourselves less than full members of this new, cobbled-together family, and disliked being assigned to the beautification of a home that we found unbeautiful in all respects, and for which we had neither natural affection nor a sense of proprietary interest.

We went to the new high school. We walked the mile down the open two-lane road on one side of which was the just-begun suburban community and on the other side of which was the cornfield.

The school was as new as the community, and still under construction for the first three years of its occupancy. One of its innovations was the notion that honesty would be engendered by the absence of security, so the lockers were designed and built both without locks and without the possibility of attaching locks. And there was the corresponding rash of thievery and many lectures about the same from the school administration, but it was difficult to point with pride to any scholastic or community tradition supporting the suggestion that we, the students, pull together in this new, utopian way. We were in school in an uncompleted building in the midst of a mud field in the midst of a cornfield. Our various sports teams were called the Spartans; and I played on those teams, which were of a wretchedness consistent with their novelty.

Meanwhile, my sister interested herself in the drama society. The year after I had left the school she obtained the lead in the school play. It called for acting and singing, both of which she had talent for, and it looked to be a signal triumph for her in her otherwise unremarkable and unenjoyed school career.

On the night of the play's opening she sat down to dinner with our mother and our stepfather. It may be that they ate a trifle early to allow her to get to the school to enjoy the excitement of the opening night. But however it was, my sister had no appetite, and she nibbled a bit at her food, and then when she got up from the table to carry her plate back to scrape it in the sink, my mother suggested that she sit down, as she had not finished her food. My sister said she really had no appetite, but my mother insisted that, as the meal had been prepared, it would be good form to sit and eat it.

My sister sat down with the plate and pecked at her food and she tried to eat a bit, and told my mother that, no, really, she possessed no appetite whatsoever, and that was due, no doubt, not to the food, but to her nervousness and excitement at the prospect of opening night.

My mother, again, said that, as the food had been cooked, it had to be eaten, and my sister tried and said that she could not; at which my mother nodded. She then got up from the table and went to the telephone and looked up the number and called the school and got the drama teacher and identified herself and told him that her daughter wouldn't be coming to school that night, that, no, she was not ill, but that she would not be coming in. Yes, yes, she said, she knew that her daughter had the lead in the play, and, yes, she was aware that many children and teachers had worked hard for it, et cetera; and so my sister did not play the lead in her school play. But I was long gone, out of the house by that time, and well out of it. I heard that story, and others like it, at the distance of twenty-five years.

In the model house our rooms were separated from their room, the master bedroom, by a bathroom and a study. On some weekends I would go alone to visit my father in the city and my sister would stay and sometimes grow frightened or lonely in her part of the house. And once, in the period when my grandfather, then in his sixties, was living with us, she became alarmed at a noise she had heard in the night, or perhaps she just became lonely, and she went out of her room and down the hall, calling for my mother, or my stepfather, or my grandfather, but the house was dark, and no one answered.

And as she went farther down the hall, toward the living room, she heard voices, and she turned the corner, and saw a light coming from under the closed door in the master bedroom, and heard my stepfather crying and the sound of my mother sobbing. So my sister went up to the door, and she heard my stepfather talking to my grandfather and saying, "Jack. Say the words. Just say the words . . ." And my grandfather, in his Eastern European accent, saying, with obvious pain and difficulty, "No. No. I can't. Why are you making me do this? Why?" And the sound of my mother crying convulsively.

My sister opened the door, and she saw my grandfather sitting on the bed, and my stepfather standing by the closet and gesturing. On the floor of the closet she saw my mother, curled in a fetal position, moaning and crying and hugging herself. My stepfather was saying, "Say the words. Just say the words." And my grandfather was breathing fast and repeating, "I can't. She knows how I feel about her. I can't." And my stepfather said, "Say the words, Jack. Please. Just say you love her." At which my mother moaned louder. And my grandfather said, "I can't."

My sister pushed the door open farther and said—I don't know what she said, but she asked, I'm sure, for some reassurance or some explanation, and my stepfather turned around and saw her and picked up a hairbrush from a dresser that he passed as he walked toward her, and he hit her in the face and slammed the door on her. And she continued to hear "Jack, say the words."

She told me that on weekends when I was gone my

stepfather ended every Sunday evening by hitting or beating her for some reason or other. He would come home from depositing his own kids back at their mother's house after their weekend visitation, and would settle down tired and angry, and, as a regular matter on those evenings, would find out some intolerable behavior on my sister's part and slap or hit or beat her.

Years later, at my mother's funeral, my sister spoke to our aunt, my mother's sister, who offered a footnote to this behavior. She said when they were young, my mother and my aunt and their parents lived in a small flat on the West Side. My grandfather was a salesman on the road from dawn on Monday until Friday night. Their family had a fiction, and that fiction, that article of faith, was that my mother was a naughty child. And each Friday, when he came home, his first question as he climbed the stairs was "What has she done this week . . . ?" At which my grandmother would tell him the terrible things that my mother had done, after which she, my mother, was beaten.

This was general knowledge in my family. The footnote concerned my grandfather's behavior later in the night. My aunt had a room of her own, and it adjoined her parents' room. And she related that each Friday, when the house had gone to bed, she, through the thin wall, heard my grandfather pleading for sex. "Cookie, please." And my grandmother responding, "No, Jack." "Cookie, please." "No, Jack." "Cookie, please."

And once my grandfather came home and asked, "What has she done this week?" and I do not know, but I imagine that the response was not completed, and perhaps hardly begun; in any case, he reached and grabbed my mother by the back of the neck and hurled her down the stairs.

And once, in our house in the suburbs, there had been an outburst by my stepfather directed at my sister. And she had somehow prevailed. It was, I think, that he had the facts of the case wrong, and had accused her of the commission of something for which she had demonstrably had no opportunity, and she pointed this out to him with what I can imagine, given the circumstances, was an understandable, and, given my prejudice, a commendable degree of freedom. Thinking the incident closed, she went back to her room to study, and, a few moments later, he threw open her door, batted the book out of her hands, and picked her up and threw her against the far wall, where she struck the back of her neck on a shelf.

She was told, the next morning, that her pain, real or pretended, held no weight, and that she would have to go to school. She protested that she could not walk, or, if at all, only with the greatest of difficulty and in great pain; but she was dressed and did walk to school, where she fainted, and was brought home. For years she suffered various headaches; an X-ray taken twenty years later for an unrelated problem revealed that when he threw her against the shelf he had cracked her vertebrae.

When we left the house we left in good spirits. When we went out to dinner, it was an adventure, which was strange to me, looking back, because many of these dinners ended with my sister or myself being banished, sullen or in tears, from the restaurant, and told to wait in the car, as we were in disgrace.

These were the excursions that had ended due to her

or my intolerable arrogance, as it was explained to us.

The happy trips were celebrated and capped with a joke. Here is the joke: my stepfather, my mother, my sister, and I would exit the restaurant, my stepfather and mother would walk to the car, telling us that they would pick us up. We children would stand by the restaurant entrance. They would drive up in the car, open the passenger door, and wait until my sister and I had started to get in. They would then drive away.

They would drive ten or fifteen feet and open the door again, and we would walk up again, and they would drive away again. They sometimes would drive around the block. But they would always come back, and by that time the four of us would be laughing in camaraderie and appreciation of what, I believe, was our only family joke.

We were doing the lawn, my sister and I. I was raking, and she was stuffing the leaves into a bag. I loathed the job, and my muscles and my mind rebelled, and I was viciously angry, and my sister said something, and I turned and threw the rake at her and it hit her in the face.

The rake was split bamboo and metal, and a piece of metal caught her lip and cut her badly.

We were both terrified, and I was sick with guilt, and we ran into the house, my sister holding her hand to her mouth, and her mouth and her hand and the front of her dress covered in blood.

We ran into the kitchen, where my mother was cooking dinner, and my mother asked what happened.

Neither of us—myself out of guilt, of course, and my sister out of a desire to avert the terrible punishment she knew I would receive—would say what had occurred.

My mother pressed us, and neither of us would answer. She said that until one or the other answered, we would not go to the hospital; and so the family sat down to dinner, where my sister clutched a napkin to her face and the blood soaked the napkin and ran down onto her food, which she had to eat; and I also ate my food, and we cleared the table and went to the hospital.

I remember the walks home from school in the frigid winter, along the cornfield that was, for all its proximity to the city, part of the prairie. The winters were viciously cold. From the remove of years, I can see how the area might and may have been beautiful. One could have walked in the stubble of the cornfields, or hunted birds, or enjoyed any of a number of pleasures naturally occurring.

Memories of Chelsea

It was the winter before I married, and I lived alone in one floor of an old row house in New York's Chelsea. I was sick all winter with a lingering cold or flu, born, I think, at least in part, from loneliness. But I also enjoyed the solitude.

Every evening—I remember it as every evening, but it cannot actually have been—I took myself to dinner at a restaurant on Ninth Avenue, and sat by myself and read novels.

I read the entire works of Willa Cather, night after night. I would eat my breaded this or that, and linger on with coffee and several cigarettes until the restaurant closed.

I was making my living as a writer for the first time in my life. A young man in his late twenties in New York, involved in and very conscious of living a romance.

I remember one Sunday in October when I washed my windows.

My apartment had four windows, and I washed them

at length on a cool, bright day, happy as I had ever been before or ever have been since.

I remember evenings in front of the fire. I had used a bearskin rug as a prop in a play of mine in Chicago, and the young woman who had lent the rug to the production later showed up in New York and made me a present of it. I'd lie on the rug in front of the fire and read, my head resting back on the head of the bear.

When I married, my wife supposed that I had made love to countless women on that bear rug, and suggested that I leave it behind. Which I did. I had made love to one woman on the rug—which story I'll tell later.

I adored that apartment. In the summer I'd sit home evenings, with a bottle of Pouilly-Fuissé, as cold as I could get it, and I'd drink and read. The wine was not expensive—this was just in advance of the vogue for white French wine—and I indulged myself.

In sum, I was self-sufficient. I was an independent young man of the world. I had an income and a future, and was beginning to have something of a name.

I was lonely on the weekends, and I remember various street fairs, cruising in search of the woman of my dreams, or, perhaps, for some other version of stability.

Weekdays I would go to the Chelsea YMCA and exercise, or I would go jog on the West Side Highway.

The elevated highway was awaiting demolition, and closed to traffic. I would jog from Twenty-third Street along the Hudson River, and, just across from the remaining passenger-ship terminals at Fifty-fourth, I would turn and jog back. On the run back I would occasionally race an ocean liner, just put out in the river and headed south. When they first started up I could keep pace with them for several hundred yards.

14

Chelsea was originally a community for the well-to-do in the shipping line. It was built for and housed ship chandlers, naval architects, captains, and others of a respectable middle-class station.

The great shipping piers spiked out into the Hudson on the west of Chelsea, two blocks from my apartment.

Ninety years before my tenure, the occupant of my house could have looked out of the kitchen window and seen that actual "forest of masts and spars."

The *Titanic,* had she docked, would have done so literally right down the street; and the reporters awaiting the survivors on the *Carpathia* drank at the bars right around the corner.

When I jogged south on the highway, I was alongside the huge deserted pier buildings, which had been appropriated for homosexual encounters and were the scene of much violence.

South of them I had a view of the Statue of Liberty, which I never saw without reciting some of Emma Lazarus's poem to pass the time and get myself a bit weepy. And I never saw the statue without feeling I was privileged to have such regular access.

Down on Eleventh Avenue was, and I hope still is, Madison Men's Shop, Melvin Madison, owner/proprietor.

I was lured into the shop by the very sturdy work clothes in the window, arranged alongside paraphernalia of the virtually defunct maritime trades—insignia, uniforms, and so on.

I became friendly with Melvin, and he allowed me to hang out in his shop, and we would chat about this and that and drink coffee.

The store had been under his command for many years.

He had quite a bit of old, unpacked, unsold, excellent, hardy, and distinctive work clothes in stock. He had jackets and caps from the 1940s, pants and shoes of a durability unimaginable in today's manufacture.

I had once spent part of a summer working as a cook on one of the Great Lakes ore boats, so I was an actual—albeit surpassingly cadet—member of the Merchant Marine, and Mel would tell me stories of his life on the ships, and of his life in the neighborhood.

Some years previous to my residence in Chelsea, I had in fact spent a bit of time around the corner from Mel's shop, frequenting the hiring hall of the National Maritime Union, trying, unsuccessfully, to get out on a ship.

Mel and his store were a focus of both romance and comfort to the south of my apartment.

To the north was Chelsea Stationers, another neighborhood landmark. It was run and owned by Ken.

Ken, and his father before him, had been in the same spot for thirty years, and they, too, had old stock in the basement.

I'd buy old 1930s report covers with happy high-stepping footballers printed on them, old pens, and legal-looking blank books in which to write. And, as either Ken or I was usually in the process of getting off cigarettes, we would bum smokes off each other and talk about women and his adventures in his community-theater group in New Jersey.

The stationery store was the first stop on my daily walk home from the Y.

As I came out of the Y, I was facing the Chelsea Hotel, long touted as a New York City literary landmark.

The Chelsea had been home to Thomas Wolfe and Dylan Thomas and Brendan Behan, and other writers no doubt drawn by their tenure there. I had, on my first visit to New York, spent a few nights there myself—a very young man terrified by the squalor and violence and noise. The hotel embodied New York to me. Nothing in my middle-class Chicago experience had prepared me for that hotel. It was not that it was, as it was, beyond romanticizing, filthy and dangerous, but that, being such, it represented itself and was accepted as a cultural landmark, and a good choice for a serious artist looking for a room.

And everyone pointed out that Virgil Thompson still lived there.

I met Virgil Thompson around the corner from the hotel, at another of my regular stops on the trek back to my apartment from the Y. I met him at Dr. Herrmann's optometrical establishment.

Louis Herrmann was a fine eye doctor and, rest in peace, a true lover of the theater.

He was Bernard Herrmann's brother and, as a kid, had actually been with Bernard in the studios for Orson Welles's "War of the Worlds" broadcast. I have never heard anyone speak more lovingly of another than Louis spoke of his brother Bernard.

He would reminisce about the Mercury Theatre, about Welles, about Bernard and Hitchcock; we would talk about the theater. Often his wife, Ruth, would be working in the office, and we would have coffee together.

He must have, at that time, been in his early sixties, and it was a revelation to me to see him with his wife, to see two people married thirty or forty years who were so obviously in love. He was a beautiful man.

Across the street from Louis was the shoe-repair store, where I would go for a shine.

That store figures prominently in my Chelsea mythology due to the interchange reported below.

I was out strolling one day with Shel Silverstein, whom I cite as my witness for the following improbable exchange.

I had broken a strap on my leather shoulder bag, and went into the shoe-repair store to have it fixed. The owner examined the bag at length, and shrugged. "How much to fix it?" I said.

"That's gonna cost you twenty dollars," he said.

"Twenty dollars?" I said. "Just to fix one *strap* . . . ?"

"Well, I can't *get* to it," he said. "I can't reach it with the machine, I got to take the bag apart, do it by hand, take one man two, three hours, do that job."

So I sighed. "Oh, all right," I said. "When can I come back for it? Thursday? Friday . . . ?"

"Naaah," he said. "Go get a cup of coffee—come back ten, fifteen minutes."

Down the street from the shoe-repair store was Kenny Fish.

Ken had a furniture store. He bought and restored and sold Grand Rapids oak. He was a superior craftsman, and he had good taste in what he bought. He was also a good companion, and I spent many hours on my way back from the gym hanging out with Ken and playing gin. He was the worst gin player I have ever met, and my home, to this day, is spotted with heavy durable furniture I won off of Kenny.

(When I left the neighborhood, Ken was still in my debt for eighty dollars or so. I found him one day, driving a hansom cab at Sixth Avenue and Central Park South. He mentioned the longstanding debt, and I suggested that he and his horse take me up to the Dakota,

18

and we would call it quits. I left him at Seventy-second Street and Central Park West, and have not seen him since.)

Next to Ken's store was Milton. He dealt in furniture and bric-a-brac, and went by the soubriquet of Captain Spaulding, perhaps because of the lyric, in the song of the same name, "Did someone call me *schnorrer* . . . ?"

Below the captain was Charlie's Laundromat.

Charlie was always good for a smoke, or to cash a small check, or to hold or relay a message for the others of the neighborhood confraternity. He was a very nice and generous and accommodating man. His daughter, he told me, married Mark Rothko's son. And he once bought me a celebratory cup of coffee when the Rothko estate won a large judgment against some art dealer.

The block also housed Joe Rosenberg and his framing establishment. Joe framed many pictures for me, and gave me two important pieces of advice. He told me never to knock wood because (he had learned after fifty years of solecism) knocking wood was an appeal (through the True Cross) for the intercession of Jesus Christ. He also told me never to marry a non-Jewish girl.

After Joe and Charlie, I rounded the corner and was almost home. I turned down the residential block, nothing between me and the necessity of actually writing save the construction of instant coffee, and a reflection, perhaps, about Clement Clarke Moore (" 'Twas the Night Before Christmas"), who at one time had lived next door.

(Anthony Perkins lived nearby, too. When I moved into my apartment I bought a clear shower–curtain liner and ordered a shower curtain to complement it. The curtain itself never arrived, so I lived with the clear liner, and that did the trick. I always wished, however, that the liner itself were enough of an oddity that someone would one day inquire why I had a clear shower curtain, and I could respond that I lived around the corner from Anthony Perkins. Well, now I have acquitted myself of it, and can get on with my life.)

In Chelsea I could look out of my living-room window and see the Empire State Building and reflect that other Chicagoans traveled 880 miles for the privilege. I could walk to the theater district or to the Village. I had a working fireplace and a pair of silver candlesticks that were the only things my grandparents brought with them out of Poland. I had a poster from the Barnum and Bailey Circus, and the bearskin rug I have spoken of before, and it is to that rug and an appurtenant misadventure connected thereto that I now refer.

To my lovely bachelor flat I had invited this very lovely young woman whom I mentioned earlier in conjunction with the bear rug. I had been pursuing her for some months, and apparently some blandishment or other worked its magic, for she finally said yes, she would come down to New York and spend the weekend with me.

She arrived in New York in the afternoon. I had promised to take her that evening to a performance of a play of mine uptown.

I took her from the station back to Chelsea, calculating that there was just enough time for some long-deferred and eagerly awaited sexual intercourse; but she said no, she'd have a bath if I didn't mind, and we could both have something to look forward to after the theater.

Well, fine. We went off, in due time, and saw the

show. As the actors were taking their final bow, I hurried her through the lobby and out onto the street.

We were in the process of getting into a cab when I heard my name called, and made the mistake of turning around.

I had been called by X, an older actor, an acquaintance of mine.

He hurried up to me, his wife close behind him, told me how much he had enjoyed the show, thanked me for the tickets, and said I didn't need the cab, as he had driven down, and we could all go back in his car.

Go back? I said. Yes. And I remembered that I had, some long weeks previously, invited him and his wife to be my guests at the show, and they had extended to me their very kind invitation to join them in their home for an after-the-theater supper.

Well. My mind raced. I had to allow him to reciprocate my gift of the tickets, and I could not, I thought (having reasoned it out as closely as I could), be so discourteous as to stand him and his wife up.

So I introduced them to my young friend, explained that she had been traveling quite a long while and was exhausted from the journey, and that we really could not stay long at their house. "Just a snack," he assured me, "and we'll send you on your way."

We got to his house. He made us a drink, and then another. I less and less subtly hinted that if we were going to eat we *should* eat, as it was getting late and my friend was very *very* tired.

He finally rose and announced that, yes, it *was* time to eat, and that, in honor of my visit, *he himself* was going to cook. And he was going to cook matzoh brei.

21

Now, gentle reader, what is matzoh brei? It is fried matzoh.

It is matzoh (that crackerlike unleavened bread) that has been soaked in egg and milk, fried in grease, and served with syrup, sugar, butter, salt, jam, or any combination of the above.

My mother, rest in peace, used to serve it on Sunday mornings. It is absolutely delicious, stupefyingly filling, and precisely the last thing one wants to eat at 11 P.M. before a scheduled night of love.

So I demurred. "Don't put yourself out," I said. And he said, "Nonsense," and cooked the matzoh brei.

He brought it out and served it heaping on my plate. And I had to eat it. Because, of course, it was an honor.

He was a Jewish Patriarch making a rare and ceremonial foray into the kitchen to cook a traditional Jewish dish to serve to me, a Young Jewish Lad, whom he had invited to his house because he was proud of me.

So I had to eat it.

I had that big, heaping plateful, and of course praised it to the skies, and so of course had to have another and a bit of a third. And I said, "That was the most delicious matzoh brei I have ever eaten."

And his wife said, *"You call that matzoh brei?"*

And *she* went into the kitchen.

And she called back that X and his family, in their ignorance, knew nothing of the nature and construction of the dish, and she started cooking her family's version of matzoh brei.

As I looked on, stupefied. I tried to leave, but X told us that we could not budge until I had made the comparison and told the world the truth.

So we sat there and waited while his wife cooked; and

I had to eat as many plates of matzoh brei as I had before, and make the ceremonial declaration of the excellence of each recipe.

I finally extricated myself and my companion, as stuffed and as sleepy as I have ever been in my life.

In the cab she told me she liked the matzoh brei.

I waddled up the stairs to my apartment, the young woman behind me, and was young enough to engage in embraces to which, at that point, neither of us was much inclined.

That is the story of the bearskin rug, and of my Chelsea apartment. I would sit by the rear window at an oak-and-steel café table, and smoke cigarettes, and look at the row of gardens running between the backs of the houses on Nineteenth and Twentieth streets. They could well have been the gardens that inspired O. Henry's "The Last Leaf."

I had no television and, for the longest time, no telephone. I had a lot of books, and, for the first time in my life, a little money. It was a romantic time.

P.Q.

In 1965 I worked for several months at a roadside diner in Trois-Rivières, Province de Quebec, on the autoroute, halfway between Montreal and Quebec City. It was there that I learned to speak a little French. There were no tourists in the city. Just the natives and sailors off of the boats that had come down the St. Lawrence to the paper mills.

I lived there in the fall. The weather was cold and damp, and, because of the paper mills, the whole town smelled like the inside of a wet cardboard box.

The diner was right on the highway. My day there ran from 10 A.M., setting up, till 1 A.M., locking up, when I'd head the two miles back down Route 2 into the town proper.

It was twenty-seven years ago, which either is or is not a long time, but seems the impossibly distant past, when I remember that I would often hitch a ride back into town on what the proprietor, Roger Bellerive, assured me was the last horse-drawn milk truck on the continent. Occasionally, I'd hitch a ride back on the street sweeper.

25

I was young and lonely, and I remember a very potent Quebec potion called simply Alcool, a clear spirit of the white lightning variety, which I bought by the shot and the pint bottle; and a poster for the latest Elvis film, *L'Amour en quatrième vitesse,* which translation I found, ethnocentrist that I was, very dilute in French.

And there was a waitress co-worker of mine who invited me to cross the river and see her home several times. I was seventeen and she twenty-four. She told me that one had only to sleep with a Quebecoise three times in order to learn the language, but I didn't go, since she seemed, at twenty-four, vastly too old for me.

The sailors came in and ordered hamburgers and root beer, and I went home stinking of grease and the Ajax I used to scrub down the griddle.

That fall I left Trois-Rivières once, to attend Yom Kippur services in Montreal, eighty miles away.

I hitchhiked down the highway in a vicious snowstorm and found myself stranded some unknown miles short of Montreal, in the middle of the storm, in the middle of the night. There were no cars coming by. I walked to a motel back down the road. The office was locked, but one of the cabins was open, so I let myself in and shivered all night under my thin coat.

The next morning I made my way into Montreal. My dress-for-temple shoes were dissolving on my feet. I found the temple and was told I couldn't get in without a ticket, and I think I probably took a bus back to Trois-Rivières. As I write, I remember a phrase from the period: that the Quebecois were a minority in Canada, and that the English were a minority in Quebec, and that the Jews were a minority everywhere. In any case, I didn't get into the temple, but what would amuse a seventeen-year-old more than a feeling of righteous wrath and misunderstood religious fervor?

A year from the next summer, several college chums and I went north to find work at Montreal's Expo '67. We were told we couldn't work in Canada without a Canadian Social Security card, and we all bemoaned the nice fat jobs going begging until one day I walked over to the Social Security office and asked them for a card, and they gave me one and, as the Brits have it, "Bob was my Uncle."

I auditioned for and got a job as an "acro dancer" with the Tibor Rudas Australian Living Screen.

Tibor's company was part of the Maurice Chevalier extravaganza, *Toutes voiles dehors!!!,* which played the Autostade at Expo '67.

The stage was in the middle of that stadium. Behind us was a drive-in–sized movie screen that was slashed vertically at intervals of one foot. A motion picture, a Parisian-street-scene drama, was projected on the screen, and at various points the cinematic characters would run toward the audience *out* of the movie and through the slits in the screen onto the stage before it.

I, as one of the acro dancers, portrayed a Parisian *apache* thug. On cue, I ran between the strips and onto the stage, where my confreres and I performed a rollicking dance, and, on cue, ran back into the screen, where our filmic doppelgängers continued the action.

At the end of the show, all of the extravaganza, which included the Barbadian Esso Triple-E Steel Band, and that's as far as my memory goes, joined Maurice Chevalier onstage and sang something or other.

I particularly remember the Esso, as they stayed in the Autostade night after night and drank Barbadian rum and partied, and on a few of those nights I was privileged to stay with them.

Expo was a treat if one worked there. The employee's pass got one straight into any of the exhibits without a wait; and, better, allowed one to stay on in the park after it had officially closed to the populace and metamorphosed into one big party.

I remember friends who, by the luck of the draw, got hired by the fair and assigned to sell programs at the main entrance of the brand-new metro—I was there on the metro's inaugural day, and stood in line and rode it. I think that is the only historical event in which I have participated. I once chatted with Howard Hughes, but I do not think that counts as "of historical significance," since it is, arguably, not important, and also since no one believes me.

In any case, friends were assigned, I say, to sell these programs at the entrance to the fair. The programs went for a buck, my friends got a 10 percent rake-off, and they were pulling down one thousand dollars, Canadian, a day. In 1967. I occasionally wonder what I would have done had I had that money at that age. I would, in my fantasies, have saved every cent and established my young self as a this or that. I would, perhaps, have bought a small business of some description and stayed in Canada. Who can say?

Well, I can say.

If I'd had that money as a nineteen-year-old, I'd have bought a car and a guitar and some clothes and partied myself into a liver condition. But I digress.

It seems that I was making three hundred or so a week

at the Autostade, and was augmenting this with my stipend for work as Johannes Gutenberg.

Yes, if you went to Expo '67, the odds are good you saw me in the West German pavilion, dressed in a leather apron and running a replica of Gutenberg's press. There I churned out printed black-letter facsimiles of Gutenberg's fifteen-something-or-other Bible, and shrugged distractedly in response to questions in many tongues.

I lived in a hovel on Ste. Catherine Street with my fellow collegians, and we plotted the formation of a new Canadian theater company. Which company almost came into existence.

I think we did some few readings in our Ste. Catherine Street apartment. I cannot remember what we may have done, but it was probably something by Beckett or Pinter, the only two writers we deemed worthy of the name in 1967.

While wandering the fairgrounds early one morning before the starting bell, I met a Japanese man. He was lost, and in some pidgin amalgam, I found out where he wanted to go and took him there. He gave me a card that explained he was the manager-director of the next world's fair, which was to be in Osaka, and he indicated that I should come work for him.

That's the prologue to my Horatio Alger story, except that as the 1970 Osaka fair approached, I was poor and friendless in Chicago or some sodding where, and could not find the magic card. And to this *day* . . .

In 1969 I was back living in Montreal, acting in a theater company at McGill University and cheerfully starving. There was a workingmen's café over near Simpson's department store that served a fresh fried trout and a short beer for one dollar, and I ate there every day, and hung around, and salted my beer to bring the foam back to it; and there was a famous and romantic bistro over on Mountain Street, the name of which I have forgotten.

I was terrible as Lenny in *The Homecoming,* and perhaps passable as the Dormouse in *Alice in Wonderland.* The theater company fell apart, I moved back to Chicago, where I wandered around looking for work, and never got to Japan.

I like the French Canadians. They have an indigenous culture and they're happy with it, they showed La Salle the way to Chicago, thus saving a million lawyers the ignominy of working on a Street with No Name, and they have always treated me more than fair.

THE WATCH

The Chicago in which I wanted to participate was a
workers' town. It was, and, in my memory, is, the various districts and the jobs that I did there: factories out in
Cicero or down in Blue Island—the Inland Steel plant in
East Chicago; Yellow Cab Unit Thirteen on Halsted.

I grew up on Dreiser and Frank Norris and Sherwood
Anderson, and I felt, following what I took to be their
lead, that the bourgeoisie was not the fit subject of literature.

So the various jobs paid my rent, and showed me
something of life, and they were irrefutable evidence of
my escape from the literarily unworthy middle class. For
not only was I a son of the middle class, I was, and
perhaps I still am, the *ne plus ultra* of that breed: a Nice
Jewish Boy. And, as that Nice Jewish Boy, I went to
college.

I went to college in the East, at a countercultural insti-
tution, a year-round camp, really, where I and those of
my class griped about the war and took ourselves quite
seriously.

The college was in the very lovely midst of nowhere in New England. It was ten miles from the nearest town; those who did not possess either an auto or a good friend with an auto were under a *de facto* house arrest on the college grounds.

I did not have an auto. My father was the child of immigrants, born right off the boat. He had sent his first-born son, in effect, to finishing school, and it never would have occurred to him to compound this enormity by supplying that son with the sybaritic indulgence of a car.

Neither would it have occurred to me to expect the same. However, I had been told, from what seems to me to've been my earliest youth, that, on my graduation from college, I'd be given a convertible.

It was not any car that I'd receive, it was *the convertible*. How this notion got started, I don't know. But my grandmother said it, and my father said it, and I looked forward to it as a fixed point in my life.

Was it a bribe, was it to be a reward? I don't know. It was an out-of-character assurance on my father's part; for he was capable of generosity, and, indeed, on occasion, of real lavishness, but both, in my memory, were much more likely to stem from impulse than from a thought-out plan. However, he had promised it, and not only had the family heard it, but we joked about it and it became, it seemed, part of our family phrase book; e.g., "Study hard, or you won't get into college, and then you know what you aren't going to get."

So much that I forgot about it. It was nothing to long for, or even, truly, to anticipate. The one event would bring about the other, as retirement, the agreed-upon pension—not a subject for anticipation, or, even, on receipt, for gratitude, but the correct conclusion of an agreement.

It was my final year at college. Graduation was to come in May, and in the preceding November I would turn twenty-one. In three and a half years at college I had learned not a damned thing. I had no skills, nor demonstrable talents. Upon graduation I would be out in the world with no money, nor prospects, nor plan. Not only did I not care, I had given it no thought at all; and I believe I assumed that some happy force would intervene and allow me to spend the rest of my life in school.

Just before the Thanksgiving break my father called. He told me he was looking forward to my return to Chicago for the holiday. Now, this was news to me, as we had not discussed my coming to Chicago, and I'd made plans to spend the long weekend with friends in the East. But, no, he said, the holiday fell two days from my birthday, and it was important for him that I be back home.

I tried to beg off, and he persevered. He pressed me to come home, and told me that it was essential, as he *had* something for me. He was sending me a ticket, and I had to come.

Well. There I was. It was *the convertible,* and my father had remembered his promise, and was calling to tell me that he was about to make good on his pledge.

I left the phone booth smiling, and quite touched. I told my friends I would be flying to Chicago, but I would be driving back. I flew to O'Hare and took a bus downtown, and took a city bus to the North Side.

On the plane and on the buses I rehearsed both my

gratitude and my surprise. Surprise, I knew, was difficult to counterfeit, and this troubled me. I would hate to disappoint my father, or to give him less than what he might consider his just due for the award of a magnificent gift.

But no, I thought, no. The moment boded well to sweep us up in sentiment free of hypocrisy on either of our parts. For was he not the child of immigrants? And was he not raised in poverty, in the Depression, by his mother, my beloved grandmother, and had we not heard countless times, my sister and I, of their poverty, and our ingratitude? And here before us was a ceremony of abundance . . . a ceremony, finally, of manhood. It was my twenty-first birthday; I was graduating from college.

I got off the Broadway bus, and walked down the side street, rehearsing all the while, and there, across from his building, was the car.

No. I had doubted. I realized that as I saw the car. No, I would admit it. To my shame. I'd doubted him. How could I have doubted? What other reason would he have had for his insistence, his almost pleading that I come back home? Of course it was the car; and I was ashamed I had doubted him. I looked at the car from across the street.

It was a Volkswagen convertible. It was a tricked-out model called the Super Beetle. It had outsized bubble skirts and wheels, and it was painted with broad racing stripes. I seem to remember a metallic black, with stripes of yellow and orange. I chuckled. I'm not sure what sort of a vehicle I'd expected—perhaps I'd thought he'd take me shopping, down on Western Avenue, and we'd be buyers together, at the horse fair. I don't know what I expected from him, but when I saw that Beetle, I was moved. It was, I thought, a choice both touching and naïve. It seemed that he had tried to put himself in the place of his son. It was as if he'd thought, What sort of car would the youth of today desire? And there was his answer, across the street.

I thought, No, that's not my style, and then reproached myself. And I was worthy of reproach. For the gift was magnificent, and, with the gift, his effort to understand me—*that* was the gift, the magnificent gift. Rather than insist that I be like him, he'd tried to make himself like me. And if my chums thought that the car was somewhat obvious, well, they could go to hell. For I was not some kid in the schoolyard who could be embarrassed by his parents; I was a man, and the owner of a valuable possession. The car could take me to work, it could take me from one city to the next, and finally, my father'd given it to me.

As I walked close to it I saw the error of my momentary reluctance to appreciate its decoration. It was truly beautiful. That such a car would not have been my first choice spoke to the defects not of the car, but of my taste.

I remember the new car sticker on the window, and I remember thinking that my dad must have expected me to come into the building by the other door, or he wouldn't have left the gift out here so prominently. Or did he mean me to see it? That was my question, as I rode the elevator up.

He met me at the door. There was the table, laid out for a party in the living room beyond. Did he look wary? No. I wondered whether to say which route I had taken home, but, no, if he'd wanted to test me, he would ask. No. It was clear that I wasn't supposed to've seen the car.

But why would he have chanced my spotting it? Well,

I thought, it's obvious. They'd delivered the car from the showroom, and he'd, carefully, as he did all things, instructed them on where it should be parked, and the car salesman had failed him. I saw that this could present a problem: if we came out of the building on the side opposite from where the car was parked—if we began what he would, doubtless, refer to as a simple walk, and could not *find* the car (which, after all, would not be parked where he'd directed it should be), would it be my place to reveal I'd *seen* it?

No. For he'd be angry then, at the car salesman. It would be wiser to be ignorant, and not be part of that confluence which spoiled his surprise. I could steer our progress back into the building by the other door. Aha. Yes. That is what I'd do.

There was another possibility: that we would leave the building by the door *near* the car, and that he'd come across it in the unexpected place, and be off-guard. But that need not be feared, as, if I stayed oblivious to his confusion for the scantest second, he would realize that my surprise would in no way be mitigated by the car's location. He would improvise, and say, "Look here!" That he'd surely have words with the car dealership later was not my responsibility.

We sat down to dinner. My father, my stepmother, my half-siblings, and several aunts. After the meal my father made a speech about my becoming a man. He told the table how he'd, in effect, demanded my return as he had something to give me. Then he reached in the lapel pocket of his jacket, draped over the back of his chair, and brought out a small case. Yes, I thought, this is as it should be. There's the key.

Some further words were said. I took the case, and

fought down an impulse to confess that I knew what it contained, et cetera, thus finessing the question of whether or not to feign surprise. I thanked him and opened the case, inside of which there was a pocket watch.

I looked at the watch, and at the case beneath the watch, where the key would be found. There was no key. I understood that this gift would be in two parts, that *this* was the element of the trip that was the surprise. I'd underestimated my father. How could I have thought that he would let an opportunity for patriarchal drama drift by unexploited.

No mention had been made of the car. It was possible, though unlikely, that he thought I'd forgotten that the car was owing to me; but in *any* case, and even if, as was most likely, I had returned to Chicago expecting the car, such hopes would indeed be dashed before they would be realized. He would make me the present of the watch, and, then, the party would go on, and at some point, he'd say, "Oh, by the way . . ." and draw my attention to the key, secreted in the lining of the watch case, or he'd suggest we go for a walk.

Once again, he would keep control. Well, that was as it should be, I thought. And a brand-new car —any car— was not the sort of present that should be given or accepted lightly, and if he chose to present the gift in his own way, it came not primarily from desire for control, but from a sense on his part of drama, which is to say, of what was fitting. I thought that that was fine.

That I had, accidentally, discovered the real present parked outside was to my advantage. It allowed me to feign, no, not to feign, to *feel* true gratitude for the watch he had given me. For, in truth, it was magnificent.

It was an Illinois pocket watch. In a gold Hunter case. The case was covered with scrollwork, and, in a small crest, it had my initials. The back of the case had a small diamond set in it. There was a quite heavy gold chain. In all, it was a superb and an obviously quite expensive present.

I thanked him for it. He explained that it was a railroad watch, that is, a watch made to the stringent standards called for by the railroads in the last century. The railroads, in the days before the radio, relied exclusively upon the accuracy of the railroaders' watches to ensure safety. Yes. I understood. I admired the watch at length, and tried it in various of my pockets, and said that, had I known, I would have worn a vest.

As the party wound down, I excused myself from the table, and took the watch and the case into a back room, where I pried up the lining of the case to find the key.

But there was no key, and there was, of course, no car; and, to one not emotionally involved, the presence of a convertible with a new-car sticker on the street is not worthy of note.

I pawned the watch many times; and once I sold it outright to the pawnbroker under the El on Van Buren Street.

He was a man who knew my father, and, several years after I'd sold it, I ran into him and he asked if I'd like my watch back. I asked why such a fine watch had lain unsold in his store, and he said that he'd never put it out, he'd kept it for me, as he thought someday I'd like it back. So I redeemed it for what I had sold it for.

I wore it now and then, over the years, with a tuxedo; but, most of the time, it stayed in a box in my desk. I had it appraised at one point, and found it was, as it looked, valuable. Over the years I thought of selling it, but never did.

I had another fantasy. I thought, or *felt,* perhaps, that the watch was in fact a token in code from my father, and that the token would be redeemed after his death.

I thought that, *after his death,* at the reading of his will, it would be shown that he'd never forgotten the convertible, and that the watch was merely a test; that if I would *present* the watch to his executors—my continued possession of it a sign that I had never broken faith with him—I would receive a fitting legacy.

My father died a year ago, may he rest in peace.

Like him I have turned, I'm afraid, into something of a patriarch, and something of a burgher. Like him I am, I think, overfond of the few difficulties I enjoyed on my travels toward substantiality. Like him I will, doubtless, subject my children, in some degree, to my personality, and my affection for my youth.

I still have the watch, which I still don't like; and, several years ago I bought myself a convertible, which, I think, I never drive without enjoyment.

The Cabin

In the cabin I liked it so it really stank. I would get the smells on my hands and all over my clothes: gun oil and kerosene for the lamps, wood smoke from the stove, and the smell of cigars over all.

Inside, the cabin was filled with the signs of decay. The log walls were darkening, the floor was aging and nicked up, the wood in the wood box was checking. Most things showed the signs of use and age, and the smoke and the oil got into everything.

Once, when I'd been away for a while, I went out to the cabin on skis, and found it disappeared—all except a foot of chimney—behind a hummock of snow. I often saw the fox standing out in the field and occasionally I saw deer in the browse at the edge of the field.

I only saw the bear once, a sow and two cubs, at the pond below the field; but I saw tracks twice more, one winter in the flower beds around the house, and one spring on the pond ice just below the cabin field.

It was too early for signs of the bear that spring, because the snow was deep, and though we'd had a day or two of thaw, we were due for at least one more month of true cold, so the bear should have been asleep; and I worried a bit for my little girl playing around the house, and put a large-caliber pistol in the kitchen, on top of the cabinet with the glasses.

The pistol lay next to two large mustard-ware bowls and two maple-sugar molds. It was pushed to the back because the child had said it frightened her. I never told her it was there.

I took it, shoved behind my belt, when I walked in the woods.

It made me feel a bit overburdened and foolish, but I knew that black bears sometimes attacked; and, though I knew these attacks to be exceedingly rare, I fantasized about being the victim of one, and of dying unarmed in deference to a mocking voice that was, finally, just another aspect of my fantasy.

In any case, one day in early fall I was walking in the woods, practicing a silent walk in preparation for hunting season.

I moved very, very slowly, lifting one foot forward, and not transferring the weight until the forward foot was absolutely and silently placed.

When you move like that, time slows down. Just as when involved in a meditation, body and breathing fit themselves to the environment, and one becomes increasingly calm and aware.

I was moving slowly through the woods, glacially, almost, or so it seemed to me, when the hair on the back of my neck stood up, and I felt something in my head, in the back of my head. Something like a shock—the physical equivalent of an intuition—and I smelled this stench, very like a skunk, though not as unpleasant, a sharp smell. And I realized that my body had frozen, and that what I was smelling was a bear, very nearby.

I heard him then, a bit behind me and to the side, moving off through the woods; and I knew he was reacting to my reacting to him, as we react when we feel ourselves observed. After the bear moved off I left the woods.

The clean smell of the winter must be like a beautiful death—like a fall from a great height: complete exhilaration.

I remember that smell in the back of my nostrils—it smelled like a "snap"—going to school on impossibly cold Chicago mornings, and I associate it with the smell of the woolen scarf wet from a runny nose and frozen to the face.

I think I was happy in those clothes because my mother was dressing me, touching me, and making me warm; and I think that must be how someone feels in the euphoria of freezing to death—that the woods are taking him home.

People say that the Indians venerated Vermont. That they worshiped, hunted, passed through, but did not make their homes there, because they held it as a sacred spot; and, indeed, many of my memories of Vermont are touched by both a joy of being alive and a consciousness of death.

Once, when I had pneumonia, I felt myself slipping into it; and, once, walking the land when I'd first bought it, carrying a survey map and a compass, I got lost. It was

February, and I was deep in the woods. I had been walking quickly, and I was warm, but the sun began to go
down suddenly, and I stopped to get my bearings, and I
became chill.

I realized that I was turned around, and consulted my
compass. In a panic, I refused to believe what it said. It
pointed one way to the road, but my recollection and
instinct pointed me the opposite way, and so I thrashed
around in the woods, my clothing wet and cold, the cold
seeping into my body as the sun went down; and, in
happy ending, stumbled, thankfully, and quite by acci-
dent, across the road. And, in the case of the pneumonia,
a friend called and came over and took me, in my three-
day delirium, to the hospital.

But one day, of course, there will be no accidental road
or antibiotic; and perhaps I delude myself, but I think that
it will feel somewhat familiar and, perhaps because of
that, somewhat less frightening, when that day comes.
And there are times when I look forward to it.

In the cabin was a dartboard. I would throw darts into it,
and, if my score surpassed a certain point, then I would
say that something I'd predicted would or would not
come to pass—depending on the agreement that I had
made with the divining dartboard prior to my throw.

But as I think back, I cannot remember what the event
(for I think it always an event of a certain type) I was
divining about was to be. It was, I think, something both
good and improbable. And I would link the ability of my
subconscious to overcome both my desire for the event
and my lack of skill, with the likelihood of the desired
event. I would, in effect, pray for grace.

And I would pray for grace through the medium of solitaire, which I would play by the hour to while away the working day. But my target shooting, another beloved activity coming under the general description of "writing"—was another matter. It was always a more serious concern, and success in it and failure both were my own fault and no added burden on the Deity.

I would proclaim to anyone around me that I had to Go and Work, and, having made the proclamation, would go off to the cabin, happy with my happy fiction. To have to work never failed to excuse me, or, so I thought, from any activity whatever.

Now: I leave for a moment the question of my feeling the need of an excuse, and address the question of superstition. I was so protective of my work, and so superstitious lest I draw the interrogation of the uninitiated and, so, anger the gods, that the only time I would refrain from the excuse of pressing work to extract me from an undesired situation was when I was actually working.

Otherwise, though—otherwise I would sit in my cabin and read or nap or throw darts or play solitaire or shoot targets; or I would smoke cigars and look out of the windows.

I would look out of the window and see the deer, or, on summer evening, see the beaver on the pond. I would look for the moose—I'd seen two moose up the road once, years ago, and others had seen them on my pond, and I felt that one day I would, too. I'd watch the ducks; I'd look for the blue heron. The heron used to return for the summer once every two years. The animals, of course, were, like solitaire, a sign of grace; and grace increased somewhat with the rarity of their appearance.

Although once I saw the mountain lion dart across the north road at dusk—like a fierce, muscular house cat five feet long—and it felt like something other than grace.

And twice in two days one summer, leaving the cabin just at dark, I heard dogs or coyotes in the woods tearing down a deer, and the sound of the deer barking, and the dogs chasing him back into the woods, and circling the cabin, and chasing back into the woods.

I would often sleep for a while at the end of the day, before I walked back to the house. Sometimes I would wake in a snowstorm. The cabin would be dark, the fire in the stove would be out finally—waking, you knew it first because you couldn't hear the hum of the fire, then you felt the cold—the wind would be pounding the west side of the cabin, coming up from the pond.

There is a calm that comes from the absence of electricity. I think the body recognizes and reacts to being encased in a structure through which electricity is flowing. I think the body, in some way, pulsates sympathetically with the electricity, and that the absence of electricity permits the reemergence of a natural calm.

This may just be my prejudice for the archaic, but I don't think so.

In any case, my cabin is heated with a turn–of–the–century Glenwood parlor stove. It is a black iron box about three feet high, two and a half feet wide, and one and a half feet deep. It sits on a small base, which rests on chubby, foliated, bombé legs that lift it ten inches or so off the floor. It has small chromed fender and chromed knobs on its front-side loading doors. It possesses a top piece called, I believe, a "victory," which is meant to rise in Victorian uselessness in a sort of inverted cup–like affair. The victory is black iron and chrome, and very impressive. I have stored it somewhere safe, and, I am sure, shall never remember where it is, let alone see it again.

The stove is both more beautiful and more useful without the ornament. It is now flat on top, and one can heat tea or burn wet socks on it, and the flat top is most useful for gauging the stove's temperature, and I refer to the different visual and auditory properties of spit on a hot stove and their application as a thermometer.

Light, when I infrequently stay past sunset, comes from various glass kerosene lamps and a few hammered-tin candle sconces. The combined smell and sound of the fire in the stove, the *thwicking* of the kerosene lamp, and the wind beating on the side wall excel all attempts to imagine it.

Next to my desk hang photographs of my four grandparents, and notes for projects long done, and for projects never done and never to be done.

The desk is an old walnut rolltop—circa 1860—with beautiful hand-carved pulls and a ratty green baize mat for writing surface. The mat is ink-stained and torn at all edges. The pigeonholes hold various memorabilia of my life and of the lives of others. Trinkets, in short.

On the desktop are several bottles of ink and a brass container made of an artillery shell and crudely engraved with the symbol of George V and the name H. STIMPSON, SOUVENIR DE LA GUERRE. I put paper clips in this box, and pens and pencils in an old Dundee marmalade container. There is a Winchester loading tool for the .38 Long cartridge, and a Colt model 1878 .45-caliber revolver, both of which function as paperweights. There is also a glass paperweight from the 1893 Columbian Exposition, and another in the shape of a horseshoe, made of pewter. The horseshoe has surmounted on the apex a crest that reads FRENCH LICK SPRINGS HOTEL: HOME OF "PLUTO," below which is written THE KENTUCKY DERBY. Also on the desk is a small rock my daughter gave me many years ago, and a ream of yellow paper.

It seems that I always have either too much or too little paper. Either I am writing in a complete frenzy, and the ream has disappeared, or I have been staring at it for months, and it refuses to diminish.

In the desk's various pigeonholes are various notepapers, a jade pig a half-inch long, an unused pocketknife issued by the Knife Collectors Association of America in 1985, a tape measure made by the Otis Elevator Company as a promotional item around the turn of the century, a medal the French government gave me for translating a play some years back, some old postcards, a pair of my eyeglasses, a blue Tiffany's box full of calling cards with my name on them.

On the wall, near my grandparents, are handprints of my two daughters, when each was aged one or so, a detective badge from New York State, and another, from Chicago, numbered twenty-six.

Stuck to the squared cedar logs of the cabin are notes and memos, a small corkboard full of commemorative pin-back buttons (Eugene Debs, Lindbergh, Roosevelt-Cox, Chicago World's Fair of 1933, Fourth Youth Aliya, for a sampling).

There is a country-checked couch and, on it, a Pendleton blanket a friend gave me. There are two wood boxes, one for logs and one for kindling. I filled them both years ago, and have left them untouched since then, as I take my wood from the large pile out on the covered porch.

On the porch are wind chimes made of hammered-out spoons and forks. My daughter gave them to me several years back on Father's Day. There is the skeleton and shell of a turtle placed on one of the ends of a log that extends beyond the square.

Many of the impedimenta in the cabin were acquired in the area at antique shops, yard sales, and auctions.

The best country auctions are the estate sales. Here the entire contents of a home—usually house, barn, and out-buildings, are taken out onto the lawn, a tent is set up, and the auctioneers dispose of it all, treasures and junk, the personal and nonpersonal, the beautiful and the awkward, to the highest bidder.

We in the audience wonder at the tenacity and perversity that would drive the human being to accumulate so much. We see objects that speak of the tastes, needs, and follies of the collector, and feel ourselves, in our contemporary and personal insights and knowledge of the worth of things, superior to that person whose goods are out on the lawn.

Some things we will treasure because of their contemporary fashion, some because of their associations for us, and some out of love for or pride in our ability to intuit the associations of the former owner.

One day, probably not in my time, but perhaps it will be, the contents of my cabin will find their way out onto the lawn, and people will marvel over the folly or the prescience of the collector; and they'll come into the cabin and probably nod to themselves in appreciation of the workmanship, and they may look at the window that, as

I write, lets in light over my left shoulder, and see the deep pencil mark at a slant across the sill, and written under it, 18 MAY.

I put the pencil mark there to show noon, on May 18, some year when I was sitting out here writing.

A Country Childhood

When I was a kid in Chicago, the country was YMCA camp. I remember the mess hall and sweating cold pitchers of milk; and I remember the kitchen boys, who were the stars of the camp community and granted every *droit de fou,* and when we were young we all wanted to grow up to be kitchen boys.

The camp was a paradise for a city kid. We had archery and riflery, and water sports off a complicated aluminum pier set out into a cold Michigan lake; and I remember several summers where my best friend, Lee, and I spent all our swimming time engaged in "water wrestling," which happy sport consisted of our attempts to drown each other.

And there were, of course, campfires, and references to the Native American in dance and crafts, and talent shows, and so on; but the distinctive feature of the camp was the trip.

We had three- and five- and twelve-day white-water canoe trips throughout Michigan, and one's status in the camp increased with age and consequent ability to take longer and more arduous trips.

I remember being in the coveted stern position of one of those heavy Grumman canoes, down on my knees, with the sand abrading my kneecaps, paddling away, with an eagle eye up ahead, and looking for the ducktails, which meant a rock in the water.

I remember the thrill of entering a race of rapids, which looked so complicated as to be incapable of navigation; and of thinking, at eleven or twelve years of age, probably for the first time in my life, Well, you are in charge—you'd better get an idea. I remember a trip where I wore my dad's World War II fiberboard helmet liner, which I had painted chrome yellow for some reason, and in which I felt, to use an expression of the period, neat. I was a gung-ho canoeist.

On the trip of the yellow helmet I pleaded with the counselor to let my canoe go last. I wanted the responsibility of being rearguard for the trip, chafing at the idea that grown-ups were following my progress and that, therefore, I was a child.

I resented the fellow's refusal to let my canoe go last. And paddled away in something of a huff and, later that day, broadsided a rock, and swamped, and got pinned between the canoe and the rock, and the fellow came along and saved me.

I lost the yellow helmet, and my pack and my sleeping bag, and, probably, one of the cute knives it was my privilege to carry to camp in those days.

We finally extracted the canoe. We borrowed paddles and made it to that day's campsite, where they told us that they knew we'd come to grief when they saw all our gear, accompanied by the yellow helmet, bobbing down the river.

I remember the eggs frying in bacon grease in the morning, and stick bread, and corn and potatoes cooked in ashes; and sassafras tea, which was advertised as, and did in fact taste something like, root beer that had been de-carbonated and altered so as to give one the runs.

On one trip we cooked those things for a week, camping in the dunes on Lake Michigan at what, I believe, was the Manistee National Forest, where the wind blew as hard and as continually as I have ever seen it. We spent the week inside our pup tents, except for the times we cooked. And sand got into everything, and we wondered if it were possible that the wind would never stop.

Once, on a hiking trip, I got lost. This trip was the feared "survival hike," which we all had to take at one point in our camp career; and when that point arrived, my cabin was told to assemble, wearing heavy clothes and carrying nothing.

On assembly, we were given one orange and one dollar each, and told to move out, that the trucks would come to reclaim us at the designated assembly point in twenty-four hours, and if we were not there when the trucks were there, the loss would be ours, as they would not wait.

So we moved out, and hiked, and when the sun went down, we ate our orange, and curled ourselves up, and got what sleep we could. I awoke very cold in the middle of the night, and looked around, and found that I was alone. There were no cabin-mates or counselors, just me in the middle of the night.

So I began to walk, and walked what must have been

eight or ten miles, following the signs to our destination, which was Manistee, Michigan. I got to town, and found the beach, which was our pickup point. The sun was coming up, and there was a diner on the beach just about opening, and they sold me several doughnuts. I watched the sun come up, happy as I've ever been in my life. Then I fell asleep.

I woke to the counselor screaming at me. It was noon. The group had just arrived at the beach. They had been searching for me since they awoke, down the road, at dawn.

I think I must have, in my anxious state, half woken in the night, and walked down the road and fallen asleep again, and forgotten my waking; so that, when I woke again, I thought my comrades had deserted me, which is when I went off in search of them.

But all was well that ended well, and I suppose I was forgiven, for when the truck came to fetch us, we sat in the open back, singing all the twenty miles back to camp, and the counselor told me that he thought that I sang well.

I spent several years at that camp. When I became too old to come back as a camper, I vowed that I would apply for the post of kitchen boy, and, so, move on to the next stage of camp life.

They made it look like such fun, scrubbing out the pots and playing mainly water-based jokes on one and all, and no one immune to their antics. But for some reason that I have forgotten, I applied for a kitchen job at a different camp, and slaved the summer away with no rest and no fun, and nothing to ennoble the experience, save that I got to live in a trailer, and that I read *Atlas Shrugged,* and *The Fountainhead,* which, like the canoe trips, was a perfect experience for a preadolescent boy.

WFMT

I grew up on the WFMT voice. It was a male voice, and full of calm, reason, and—most important, I think—self-esteem. The voice seemed to say: "This is the way we do things here. The music we play, the shows we air—we are proud of them. They reflect our vision of the world."

That WFMT diction, which we, in acting school, called Middle Atlantic speech, those endless WFMT pauses, were (and still are) the sound of home to me. I would be traveling or living in the East and switch on the car radio and hear, "And now . . ." and it would be some local FM station rebroadcasting the Chicago Symphony Orchestra, and those two words would link me to home.

As a teenager, the big event of my week was listening to *The Midnight Special*. I would go over to my friend's house near the Midway in Hyde Park, and we teenagers would sit from the opening of Leadbelly singing "The Midnight Special" through John Jacob Niles singing "Lonesome Valley," which, in those days, was followed by the sign-off. We would sit entranced.

The program *was* Chicago. It was the Chicago of the

living culture of the mind. The Chicago of Hutchins, and the tradition of free thought: the Hyde Park tradition of Thorstein Veblen and Clarence Darrow, of Vachel Lindsay, of Dreiser.

The idea in the air was that culture was what we, the people, did. The idea was—and is—that we were *surrounded* by culture. It was not alien to us. It was what the people did and thought and sang and wrote about. The idea was the particularly Chicagoan admixture of the populist and the intellectual. The model, the Hutchins model, the Chicago model of the European freethinker, was an autodidact: a man or woman who so loved the world around him or her that he or she was moved to investigate it further—either by creating works of art or by appreciating those works.

The very catholicity of the *Special* was instructive to us: blues, folk music, show tunes, and satire, as the lead-in has it. What better way to spend Saturday night, or one's life, for that matter?

Our heroes, we who grew up listening to the *Special,* were those with vast talent and audacity, and no respect: Shel Silverstein, Lord Buckley, Mike Nichols, Gibson and Camp, Studs Terkel . . .

We delighted in living in the same neighborhood in which Severn Darden first gave Professor Walter VanDer Vogelveider's "Short Talk on the Universe," in which he informed a theretofore ignorant world that, yes, fish think, but not fast enough. In the same neighborhood that housed the Compass Players, whose scions, Nichols and May, we would hear on the *Special* with regularity.

We would play at guessing which selection Ray Nordstrand or Norm Pelligrini, the program directors, would play next. Oh, he's just played Beyond the Fringe's cut of "two miners," next he'll most likely play Cisco Houston's "Dark as a Dungeon," or perhaps Pete Seeger's "Miner's Life." We played along, and were, if memory serves me, regularly correct in our guesses. It was our culture. We stayed up all night New Year's Eve with the *All-Night Special,* and called in our requests and comments. It was ours. Like the symphony, or the lions in front of the Art Institute, or the August sickness of the Cubs. WFMT was Chaliapin singing the "Song of the Volga Boatmen." It was Ray Nordstrand saying, "The time in Chicago is [*pause*] eleven [*pause*] fifteen [*interminable pause*] . . . a little later than usual"—one of the most bizarre utterances I have ever heard on the radio, and yet his reading rendered it perfectly comprehensible.

WFMT announcers, speaking of which, are the only people I have ever heard who have the capacity to read a phone number as if they were stating a philosophic proposition: I don't think I can do it justice in print, but you know what I'm talking about. They'd read it as if it were a syllogism: that number is four seven *two* ["If *A*"] . . . six three [". . . and now I will conclude my argument"] nine [*short pause*] four. . . [Then *B*: QED"].

I once asked Norm Pelligrini how the station managed to train its announcers, how it schooled them to the high level of recognizable uniformity and clarity. He told me that the station didn't train the announcers at all, that they "just got the idea."

WFMT meant listening to Studs and his humanism and enthusiasm and, finally, delighted *wonder* at the whole damn thing. Later on in my life it meant going down to the studio and doing the show with Studs—with him and me reading a part of some new play of mine, and him always choosing the flashy role.

Most arts organizations decay and stink before they die. Most of them have outlived their allotted span of days, their healthy usefulness, long before they are threatened by this or that encroachment.

Most arts organizations are short-lived.

WFMT has lived long and has served and continues to serve the community in an essential way. It has persisted and grown.

I have been living outside of Chicago for many years, and can only assume that keeping the station reflective of its directors' individual and collective vision has not, at times, been easy or pleasant.

The station sounds to me today much as it did when I was a kid: a voice saying, " *'Culture'* is just that which we do. Here are some things in our heritage which we enjoy, and we think you will enjoy them, too." It was and is a beautiful voice, a self-respecting voice, and the voice of home.

Cold Toast

I once had a play running in the West End of London. The show, a production with an American cast, was sold out and threatening a very long run. I came over a few weeks into the run to visit and, I suppose, to bask in the success of the play. I ran into one of the actors on the street. "Isn't it *great*?" I said. "The damn thing's going to run forever."

"I'm going home next week," he said. And there was a pause. "The whole cast is going home next week."

"Why?" I asked.

"Because," he said, "we're homesick."

Well. They did go home. And I understood it completely.

I myself tend to get homesick in London. Because it is home and it is most definitely *not* home. For example, try as you will, you cannot remember the arcane rules of pub hours, and, thinking that you have finally figured it out, are forever going into a pub hoping for a drink and not to be again rebuffed, only to be greeted by a waitress looking you in the eye and proclaiming in what probably is

not, but seems to be, an air of paternalistic disappointment, "Two-nineteen," or some such, or whatever time
it happens to be when you get into the pub and the pub
has just closed, and you have no drink and are far away
from home.

So, also, with the wrong-side-of-the-road. Tired, jet-
lagged, usually dyspeptic from the constant balancing act
of too much tea, too much liquor, not enough sleep, you
are forever coming up to the intersection and thinking:
Ah, yes, you only look the opposite way from the way
you were *going* to look, and then . . . Only to step off the
curb and invariably be looking the wrong way—which,
when coupled with the laudable directness of the London
driver, can make life for the expatriate pedestrian no joke;
and, in fact, a colleague of mine was most certainly killed
on a London street as he stepped off looking the wrong
way.

And why dyspeptic? Your stomach is out of whack
from the time change, and what is there to eat?

In the States, and in a peripatetic business, one spends
one's life eating restaurant and hotel food. After a few
weeks in any one hotel, after a few years in all of the
hotels, all restaurant and hotel food tastes the same. It
tastes like "food," and food tastes like something to be
gotten down so that one may have eaten it, and the best
one can say of most of it is that it is (when it is) hot. My
friend Greg Mosher and I, transported Chicagoans, spent
years working in the New York theater. We were
charmed by the compartmentalization of New York,
how, in this most materialistic and commercial of cities,
whatever object one required, there was not only a store
that sold it, but a district that housed many stores of that
ilk. To wit: the fur district, the trimmings district, the

flower district, et cetera. And Greg and I took to joking, whenever one or the other would require a particularly arcane item, for example, a shooting stick, "Oh, get it in the shooting-stick district." Or, to belabor the joke, as it was one we loved, cherishing habit at least as much as humor, the dental-floss district, or, for example, when at the dentist, "I'm calling from the heart of the root-canal district." We always referred to London as the cold-toast district. And we would remark to each other that in America, where anything new is good, and anything new and foreign is doubly good, never have we seen or could we imagine a sign that advertised BRITISH COOKING.

There are many many fine things about Great Britain, and London in particular. None of them are the cooking, and I don't think most Londoners could identify a vegetable with a gun to their head.

Greg was over in London directing a play of mine. He'd been there for some weeks. I came over, and we had breakfast; we met in the restaurant of the hotel, and I spied on the menu HOT BUTTERED TOAST, and grinned and turned the menu around to show Greg, who did not laugh. "Let's order it," I suggested merrily, but he did not laugh, and he did not laugh when the toast arrived, cold as earth, limp, and sodden. And the look in his eyes said, "After a month, it is no longer funny."

London and the States seem much the same, but they aren't. England is, of course, a different world. It has its own abundant courtesies and gentlenesses, but they are different from ours over here, and after a while, to us Murrcans, it gets wearisome, and we want to go home.

What do I do for comfort while I am there? I do as the Romans do and drink a lot of tea. I can't figure out when to get into those poncy pubs, but I adore the invitingness and accessibility of the various tea shoppes, and here follows a survey of comfortable and relaxed times drinking tea in London.

EMBANKMENT

I am walking down along the Embankment. I have slept much too late, because of the jet lag, and am betwixt and between. I am due at the theater in an hour and a half, not enough time to write or do anything serious, just enough time, I decide, to take a long walk. I walk from my hotel down Piccadilly, down to the mobs of Continental tourists at Piccadilly Circus, down past one of my favorite tea shoppes on a street I believe is called Haymarket, but I believe that because it houses a theater called the Haymarket, so I am elaborating the trappings of my profession into a general rule, but so do we all.

I once had the most delicious afternoon in this shoppe, having been dreadfully jet-lagged—as, in fact, I am now—and was soothing myself with gallons of their tea hot beyond hot, not only the hottest beverage possible, but the hottest thing on earth. This tea did not grow cooler over time, as I sat outside in a very chill London afternoon, but stayed hot as it was, hot enough for Vulcan, and, if that can be true, cannot it be true that the tea, sitting out, actually grew hotter? Yes. It can. And I watched a Scandinavian couple at the table next to me on the street. They were very attentive to each other, and I was fond of them.

It seems to me that I also wrote something on that afternoon, and I probably was fond of what I'd written. In any case, I cherished this, my tea shoppe near the

Haymarket Theatre, when I was disoriented, and cold, and knew no one, and had no idea what nuances of behavior meant in this strange land, and I was, in effect, as a ghost, who could see and not be seen because he was not there.

This day, though, I did not stop at this magic shoppe, for fear that it would not be the same; as, of course, it would not. Why, I thought, should I subject the current foreign couple or couples who would, no doubt, be there, to unfair comparison with my charmed Scandinavian pair in their leather jackets, who had, doubtless, retired to the north to pursue some incredibly romantic and important series of tasks?

I gave that shoppe a pass, and wandered in what I believed was the general direction of the Embankment, from which place I knew I could always turn to the left, and walk till I came to Waterloo Bridge, and then over the bridge to the theater.

I became disoriented, and found myself in front of some palace or other. There were two members of the Life Guards, up on their matched blacks. Imposing spectacle. These monsters in Hessian boots and plumed helmets, heads fifteen feet in the air, unmoving. What a magnificent thing, I thought. The one on the left gave a signal of some kind, and a foot soldier in the middle stamped, executed a right turn, and slow-marched over to the horsemen, where they held a stiff and military colloquy for a moment about what I assumed was girls.

The faces of the two were beautifully English, round and ruddy and open. The nature of their faces, and, in fact, their silhouettes in the plumed helmets, were identical to those of the London skinheads: choked, ruddy faces, spiked hair to increase height and refer to the equine and inspire something on the continuum from respect to terror. The skinheads and the Life Guards both proclaim, "I am bigger than you, and I subscribe to a code so superior to yours as to enable me to commit any violence. You do not exist for me."

I looked at these boys on their horses and was myself sufficiently awed by them as to find this thought springing into my mind: Yes, boys, but we whopped your ass fairly roundly in 1778, then, *didn't* we . . . ?

And on that craven note of borrowed courage, I walked on and eventually discovered both the Embankment and a great hunger.

I had a half hour before the theater curtain, and I sat down at a café facing the Thames. Tourist buses from Germany and France were filling up at the curbside, the café was closing, and nobody wanted to serve me, so I got up after ten minutes and discovered a take-out tea shoppe next door, where I bought a tasteless apple confection of some sort, mostly paste. I wolfed it down gratefully, and walked down the Embankment, trying to clean the remnants of the sticky paste off my hands, and holding a piping-hot Styrofoam cup of tea. There was a sidewalk artist working on a pastel of a snake charmer. I heard or read somewhere that these men learned one scene by rote, and then went around drawing it on the sidewalk in chalk for the rest of their lives, the one picture that they knew.

I watched this man putting far-beyond-finishing touches on his snake charmer. The day was cold, there was pitifully little money in his hat, and he smoothed and resmoothed the border of his scene belligerently. I wanted to ask him if he knew only this one picture, but he radiated defiance. I threw some money in his hat and walked on. I felt a bit strange drinking on the street, a very un-British thing to do. The tea was wretched in any case, and tasted terribly of Styrofoam. I emptied the tea into the street, and threw the cup into a trash basket.

I walked past monuments on the Embankment, all to the dead. Not TO OUR HEROES, but to THE DEAD, the dead of the navy, of the air force. A lovely monument to the dead of the air force in the Great War, with a pathetic addendum engraved on the pedestal, homage to the dead of the next Great War a scant twenty years later.

There was a beautiful sculpted group—a mother herding her children—from A GRATEFUL BELGIUM. Her neck seemed out-of-drawing, until seen from the side, where we got the benefit of her great solicitousness.

I climbed the stairs up from the Embankment, at Waterloo Bridge. On the landing, someone had spray-painted I HATE . . . And I climbed eagerly to see, as the view permitted me, what it was, in London, that one hated. I expected the traditional "niggers," or "faggots," or perhaps, "kikes," and was rather surprised to find THE POLICE.

Over Waterloo Bridge I went, and over to the National Theatre, and being some minutes early, to one of their great cafés for a cup of tea.

CAMDEN TOWN

I am on a mission, to get my laundry done. I also want to go see all the old clothes in Camden Town.

It is a very rainy Saturday. I stuff my small clothes in my knapsack and set out for Camden Town by cab. The knapsack is a small black affair, and I have sewn onto it the patch of my partner's film company, Filmhaus. The patch has a cow staring at a camera, and the legend NEW YORK/MONTANA. The sack is full of soiled underthings, and the presence of this most mundane phenomenon reassures and encourages me as I venture out into Unknown London.

It is too cold and rainy to look at old clothes. The streets are mobbed with young people in Harley jackets, looking in at the stalls and shops, looking for that last perfect article of attire, that perfect suggestion which will complete them. I understand completely, and agree with Mr. Shaw that there is no peace in the world which surpasseth the peace of knowing that one is perfectly dressed.

These people on the street are all twenty years younger than I. I remember myself at their age, scrounging the thrift stores of Chicago, looking for the perfect leather jacket (then priced around five dollars if one got lucky at Goodwill Industries), the perfect Harris Tweed overcoat (twenty-five cents—that's right), the perfect barely worn white cotton shirt for a dime. That was our uniform in the sixties, as "children of the sixties," and well into the seventies as empowered by our profession of the theater to dress casually in all circumstances. And there I was, twenty years later, and still pursuing, in Camden Town, that vision of elegant tragedy first promulgated by Mr. Brando and James Dean. No, I tell a lie, and have committed that solecism of the nonprofessional—the actors just wore the clothes, the designer *created* the clothes. And, as I most certainly feel that when the time comes for me to write my theatrical memoirs, the world will be far past being able to print them, let alone appreciate them, I will share a memory of a dinner party in Cambridge, Massachusetts, 1988. The guest of honor was Lucinda

Ballard, costume designer of *A Streetcar Named Desire,*
Cat on a Hot Tin Roof, The Sound of Music, Showboat, The
Glass Menagerie, and many other Broadway shows, and
the creator of many American looks. I was her dinner
partner, and asked her first, as, I am sure, many had done
over the years, about Brando and his torn T-shirt in *A*
Streetcar Named Desire. And she told me that it had come
to her in a flash, that each T-shirt was hand-stitched to
form to his torso, that each shirt was hand-dyed a
washed-out pink, and that she personally distressed (that
is, created artificial signs of wear) each shirt with a razor
blade until she got the desired effect. So credit where
credit is due. And here we were forty or so years after the
fact (*Streetcar* opened on Broadway in 1947), longing for
that grace of Brando, and seeking it in sainted relics. I
was dressed like every Limey bloke on the high street in
Camden Town. As they were younger than I, they were
a bit more driven to get out in the rain and find themselves through clothing. Or perhaps I had just become
over the hill and had given up. But give up for the day I
had, and I found a Laundromat, and changed some pound
coins for coins of ten shillings, and deciphered and em-
ployed machines to sell me soap, and got the laundry
going, and felt quite proud of myself.

Down the side street was a shop that sold "aeronautical
models," and I looked in the window at the lovely things;
I so adored them as a kid—those balsa-wood gossamers,
those "thoughts," which, powered by a gasoline engine
the size of one's thumb, took to the air. I suppose
"planes" is the word I am looking for, and what American could walk through London without thinking of
planes? No one who had ever been an American boy in
the fifties, in any case.

I stopped in at the Penguin bookstore, always charmed to see the different formats and titles of the books. Books in our Benighted States are getting so regimented, aren't they? Fewer individually owned bookstores every year, less publication of the out-of-the-way or the questionable, and the benevolence of any present oligarchy must inevitably, must it not . . . oh well.

I bought a book by T. H. White, *The Goshawk,* a memoir of several months White spent in the English countryside in 1939, training a large hawk with the aid only of a three-hundred-year-old manual. I took the book around the corner to an Italian eatery—prices scribbled on slate on the walls, very much a "lunchroom," we would say in the U.S., or a "luncheonette." Many students inside, reading, talking, eating what looked like and proved to be good hot food. I had a pizza "Neapolitan," a designation the translation of which I cannot remember, but which I do remember was quite good. And I had, of course, a lot of dark hot tea, and the waitress suggested something for dessert that I could not understand, and no amount of repetition clarified it for me. After a pause, she averred: "It's like a sponge," and I decided to pass.

I bought a copy of *Time Out,* the nightlife magazine, and took it back to the Laundromat, where I put my clothes into the dryer, then looked for something to do.

I found a film I wanted to see at the ICA, the Institute of Contemporary Art, that evening, and called my friends Dick and Laura, Americans who had just shown up most unexpectedly in London, and we planned to meet at the ICA in an hour.

I got a cab in the rain, and he took me down to the ICA on the Mall. It took a bit to get there, and the cabbie kept circling, and eventually leaned back to explain, "We seem to be caught in a one-way scheme," so I got out, after asking directions, and walked under some rig that looked like the Brandenburg Gate, and arrived, in fifty yards, fairly wet, at the ICA.

I browsed in their bookstore, and looked at a bunch of Soviet paintings by Erik Bulatov. Very serious things they were, too, quite poster-presentational and dealing, it seemed, with life in Soviet society. How fine, I thought, to live in an environment in which it is not incumbent upon things to *mean* anything. And there were very serious and attractive young men and women in the ICA café, playing chess and looking at one another. They could not have been more skinny, or have smoked tobacco more beautifully. We do not have their like in my land anymore. I, of course, drank tea, although my teeth were floating; but, like driving cross-country, it is easier to continue than to stop. Dick and Laura showed up. We found that the film we wished was off, I had misread *Time Out;* and some Eastern European semianimated thing was showing. We were wet Americans and had had enough meaning for the day, and so trooped over to Leicester Square and bought tickets for a late showing of *Dangerous Liaisons,* and killed the time before the show by going to a French restaurant across from the Duke of York's Theatre and getting very very drunk, after which I believe we went to the film.

ISLINGTON

Much of my tourist career in London is spent waiting. I am out of sync with the life around me. Jet lag, sleeplessness, and cultural differences have unstuck me from any routine that could possibly be indigenous to the surroundings, and I spend a lot of time waiting for an event to occur, waiting to fall asleep, waiting for the city to come to life, waiting for friends to finish work. Today I am waiting in Islington. I don't know where much of anything in London is in relation to anything else, but since the taxi has not crossed the Thames, I suppose that Islington is to the north.

We drive through an area of antique shops, which disposes me kindly toward it. I love antique shops and antique districts, as they are, to my eye, a sign of healthy organic decay—usually of a lower-class district that has fallen on even harder times and is no longer capable of supporting its citizens, but offers very low rent to junk dealers. The junk dealers are supplanted by their high-rent artistic counterparts, and the antiques draw the adventuresome upper classes, who eventually gentrify the area with their very own abodes. A civilization eating and being eaten. Sounds good to me.

I am also, by nature and profession, a browser, and so feel very much at home in an area devoted to browsing. I have several hours to kill while friends finish a recording session in Islington.

I walk down the street and buy a FREE NELSON MANDELA button from a shop devoted to books and memorabilia supporting the ANC. I walk down the road through the midst of the antique stores in the high street, but they are all closed on this particular day.

Farther up the high street are stores selling "retro" American clothing, and I mark down a tour of that enclave for the end of the day. But now I have found, one could hardly call it a tea shoppe—it is a hole-in-the-wall with four tables and an espresso machine in back. The radio is blaring, there are signs all over the walls about Irish events. Many of them refer to boxing. The woman behind the counter has an Irish accent so thick I cannot understand a single word she is saying, and no more can she understand me. I point to items on the menu, tea, minestrone soup, and toast. She nods.

I take a seat in the front of the place; sunlight is streaming over the road. Across the street is the Islington library. It is open today. I feel a great sense of security. Here are, in fact, two places in which I can write if I so choose. I have the T. H. White book in my bag, my notebook and pen and ink are in the bag, this Irishwoman is about to bring me tea. The afternoon is, in effect, perfect. *Even should the tea shoppe be forced to close,* by some terrible mischance, I am free to go across the street and sit in what will certainly prove to be the most excellent library, and hang out there, a perfectly content man.

She brings the tea. It is the best tea I have ever had in my life. She brings the soup. It is red water with two noodles in it. I smell it, and it smells like the food in prison. I drink it anyway. The toast is actually hot, and buttery, and I have two orders. I start working on a poem about a dream I had the previous night.

The dream is one I have been having all my life. I am climbing a hill and, as I climb, the hill becomes steeper and steeper. I cannot walk another step. I have to make it up the hill, but I cannot climb. Why does the hill become increasingly steep? This is my recurring dream. I have had it hundreds of times. The night before, however, there was a change in the dream, the first change ever. I stopped halfway up the hill, and rested, and was joined by my stepmother and a beautiful naked young girl, who reclined on the grass and smiled at me.

The change in the dream is, to me, a great reprieve, and I am absorbed in writing for two hours. Drinking tea the while. When I look up, it is beginning to get dark in the high street, and I am almost late for my meeting.

I pay up and leave the little shoppe, and start off for the recording studio.

I can't resist stopping off at one of the used-clothing stores on the way. The gent behind the counter admires my leather jacket and asks where I bought it. (Vanson Leathers, Quincy, Massachusetts.) He asks what it cost and I tell him. I browse through his long-traveled American goods. He has a nice selection of stuff made by the Pendleton mills. I firmly believe that nothing in the world is better than an old wool Pendleton shirt that has been worn and loved and cared for and broken in over the years. Nothing is more comforting or more comfortable. The shirts he has on his rack are all these things, but they are too small. They are also cut on some strangely un-American pattern. The salesman tells me that they were a special order Pendleton did for Germany in the fifties. No, not for mine. And not for mine loden cloth. "Thank you very much, I'm sure," as they say here.

I hurry down the streets, armed with directions and a copy of *London A to Zed,* and find the recording studio, which is nestled in the back of an old church in a building that was probably the rectory.

The band is due to conclude recording at seven. But having lived my life in show business, I know better. I arrive at seven-fifteen and have my book to occupy me until they conclude their session at midnight, when we all go home.

CHELSEA FARMERS MARKET/THE KINGS ROAD

Today I am meeting some actor friends for lunch. They are rehearsing on Old Church Street, "down by the Embankment end." So down I go to someplace called Pytet House. Inside everyone is smoking tobacco (very refreshing, as virtually all of us Yank theatrical types have given it up), and talking trash and history in order to avoid rehearsing the play.

The same the world over. I feel right at home, and settle back in the shadows. On the wall are paintings of the various houses on Old Church Street. I notice that the one supposedly next door to this Pytet House in which I now find myself was the home of George Eliot.

The actors muck about for the best part of an hour, and we all go off to lunch. I pass by the house where Eliot supposedly lived, but find neither the number indicated by the drawing nor a plaque commemorating her presence there; and how would I have known, I wondered, even *had* I found it, if it was the house of her unhappy marriage, or the house of her content cohabitation with Mr. Lewes? What a potential misstep you have been saved from, I thought—just think if you had waxed all sentimental over an abode in which your beloved Ms. Evans was miserable. We all troop off to the Chelsea Farmers Market, a surpassingly quaint collection of shops a couple of blocks away. We pass a palm reader, a perfumer, and then settle in a very good health-food restaurant, and we all have baked potatoes and tea and tell theatrical stories from two sides of the Atlantic and arrive back at the rehearsal hall ten minutes late. I am invited back to watch more rehearsal, but no, I have had enough Art for the day, and long for Life. I plead a previous engagement.

I hurry back to the palm reader. He sits me down and tells me my life story.

He tells me that these are the best years of my life. That I am in the process of changing everything that I believe in, that I feel frustrated, alone, frightened, and unsure, and what a wonderful thing this is. This period is wonderful, he explains, because God is protecting me. God is shielding me and preventing me from making a misstep. I try to go right. I cannot go right, I try to go left, I cannot go left. I will look back on this year, he says, as the luckiest year of my life.

I drink in this information so gratefully. He goes on for an hour. I know he is giving me a stock "crossroads" reading; that he will give the same reading to virtually everyone who comes into his shop. I know that people come into his shop because and only because they find themselves at a crossroads. I know all these things, and I don't care. I drink it in. I thank him. I pay him. I walk out of his shop, out of the Chelsea Farmers Market, and I feel drained but good.

I walk down the Kings Road, past thousands of shops that all seem to be selling leather jackets.

I feel inspired to live through this year gratefully and, if I can, gracefully. I wander into Rylands stationery store and buy a new notebook, with the humble hope that I may write things in it that will be well done.

I am enchanted by the stationery store. I love office

supplies. With their exception, everything in my line of work takes place in my head, which is to say, it is arguable whether it occurs at all. Office supplies are the only artifacts, and the choice of a pen or a notebook is a big deal to me. I discover very cunning medium-sized lined, bound notebooks. I suppress the urge to buy many (if I buy many I will feel taxed with filling them all, and I will become discouraged). I buy one and walk back out on the Kings Road.

I have a wretched cup of tea in some French patisserie-chain outlet. I find that I am exhausted—probably by my hour with the reader. I take a cab back to my hotel.

THE GOSHAWK

That evening I go to the theater. And, after the theater I am alone.

In my hotel I take off my suit jacket and hang it neatly in the closet.

I set myself up at the desk in the hotel room. I prop my feet up on the desk and lean back. I am going to finish the T. H. White book.

This is one of the best books I have ever read in my life. The prose is hard and clear as a crystal. It is unsentimental, it is simply written, it is a delight and an inspiration. I read for several hours. I get up to open the French windows onto the street. It is now around two in the morning. I order tea and burnt toast from room service.

The tea arrives. It is the middle of the night. I am reading about the training of the goshawk. I am sharing Mr. White's experiences. I *myself* now want to capture and train a hawk. I want to live a simple and a pure life. I want to confine myself to the wind and the rain, and make the body and mind of a hawk the complete focus of my existence. However, I will gladly settle for sitting in this hotel room in London with my book and cup of tea.

THE TRUCK FACTORY

I can't remember the exact year, but it was sometime in the mid-sixties. Either I was home from college or it was the last summer before I went away. I had a job at the truck factory.

I was living with my dad near the lake, and the truck factory was out near Cicero. I got there and back by riding with a couple of Swedish guys. I think I paid them a dollar a day, or it might have been a dollar a trip. In any case, halfway through the summer they decided to up the ante on me, and I remember the close and rather vicious expression on their faces when they informed me of the fare increase.

I started out my day around 5 A.M. It was still something other than unbearably hot on the street, and I remember running into the same paperboy every morning on Broadway around Addison, and thinking, as I nodded to him, what a beautiful place the world was. I smoked a cigarette at the bus stop on Addison, and waited for the bus.

The bus took me way the hell and gone out west, to the place where I would wait on the corner for my ride.

The two Swedish guys, picturesque and improbable as this seems, referred to me throughout the summer as "The Rider." I was The Rider. And I rode in the back. The car was a '55 Chevy in mint condition. They picked me up on Madison, and we rode at about thirty miles an hour out west to the factory. The ride burned me up every day, out and back. If they would have driven at the speed limit, I could have slept another half hour in the morning, I could have been home half an hour earlier and had a shower and a beer. The slowness of the ride seemed to me to be an expression of their hatred for the world.

We had to punch in before seven-thirty. It wasn't hard to do because we were always early. Another of the great moments in the day was that which came after punching in and before work. There was time for another cigarette and a cup of coffee from a vending truck. To this day I love those vending trucks with the quilted silver sides. I think everyone must.

I worked in the maintenance department, which meant that I went where they sent me and did what they told me to do when I got there. My favorite job of the summer was testing torque rods. I am not sure what torque rods do, but I know that these torque rods were around two and a half feet long and had a weld at each of their ends, and that this batch had been welded incorrectly. So I was placed in a corner of the factory with barrels of torque rods. I took them, one by one, out of their barrel, first placed one and then the next weld on an anvil, and whacked the welds with a sledgehammer, in an effort to get the welds to part. I did that for several days, and there was something about the rhythm of the job—flipping the torque rod in the air to get to the weld on the other side, whanging the thing—that was completely satisfying.

I spent a month about twenty feet above a concrete floor, ripping out an asbestos ceiling.

A hangarlike part of the truck factory was being renovated, and I and a few others in the maintenance department were commissioned to get the ceiling down. We spent each day duck-walking on two-by-six joists twenty feet up in the air, as I have said, ripping the old ceiling out with pry bars. For many years I had less than strong lungs, and fairly raspy breath, and I would like to attribute those conditions to the month spent with the asbestos, which seems to me a more dramatic story than twenty-five years of tobacco.

There was another month spent with weed killer and a backpack spray canister. I roamed the outskirts of the factory, spraying that which passed for grass. At one point I lost the nozzle for the apparatus. I can't remember how or why, except that it was an act of negligence on my part. I remember being bored, and thinking, Oh, hell, I know I should do (a) with this nozzle, and it would be just as easy to do (a) as to do otherwise, but I will do (b) because I am bored, and perhaps this will make someone pay.

Soon after being transferred out of the weed job, I was called before a tribunal of my superiors and asked what became of the nozzle. I, of course, lied and told them I had no idea. I remember that the tribunal went on for a godlessly long time, at the end of which one of the senior men in the maintenance department said, "Well, I *believe* him. I *believe* him, and that's that." And I thought, You dumb sonofabitch, of *course* I lost the nozzle. Everyone here *knows* that except *you*. . . .

Why was the nozzle that important to them? I don't know. Why did they not just dock me whatever dollar or two it cost and be done with it? I don't know. I remember getting docked for various other things. I was docked for punching out early, for example, and for punching in late at the end of lunch.

Lunch was twenty minutes, whistle to whistle. When the whistle blew I was sodden with sweat and exhausted. Many days I would climb into the bunk of a sleeper cab and fall asleep. I remember them as the deepest sleeps of my life. I loved those sleeper cabs. I recall one of the factory hands gesturing to a matched pair of ready-to-roll tractors and telling me, "Son, inside of a year, one of them is going to pay for the both. . . ." And when he told me, I wanted to be picking up those tractors, to be putting them out on the highway, and having one pay for the both inside of a year. I wanted to be sleeping in the back of the cab as the truck rolled down the highway. I can't imagine anyone who wouldn't.

One day they were digging a trench along the outside of the main factory building, and a couple of guys (I would like to say that they were from the maintenance department, but I don't know if that's true) were down in the trench; just before lunchtime, the trench fell in on them, and they died. I think I found out about it after lunch. I was most probably napping.

There was some sort of chemical factory on the far side of the truck factory, and when the wind blew toward us, which was much of the time, everything smelled as I think hell must smell. Inhuman, and contrived, and unhealthy beyond mistake.

What else happened that summer? I put a nail through the sole of my workshoe, and had to get a tetanus shot, and I limped for a week or so, and learned about steel-soled shoes.

I argued one long week with myself about taking a Friday off. The Monday was a holiday of some sort, and you were paid for it if you worked the two adjoining workdays. I had some important appointment and, of course, I didn't go in on Friday, and so lost the holiday pay, and am still upset about it twenty-five years later, and still do not know whether to be mad at myself for my weakness, or at the factory for coming up with such a good plan for ensuring attendance.

The trucks were made to order, and had a reputation for being top of the line.

I've seen them on the road in the Midwest or, infrequently, in the East, and invariably say to anybody in the car, "You see that truck? I used to work there."

In Vermont

The term that comes easiest to mind is *ghosts,* but the lights on the hill weren't ghosts, or, if they were, I am not sure what ghosts are; as, of course, I am not one. I can't say what they are, but I knew when I encountered them.

And the hill itself may have had something to do with it. Down at the bottom, near my house, there is the graveyard; and I was thinking about Annie's story on the night I passed it, coming home, and something pulled my coat.

I'd like to say that I "felt something," which is to say, some presence, but all I felt was the tug on my coat sleeve. I was walking dead on the crown of the road. The night was pitch dark, and I was on the crown to avoid any possibility of branches whipping my face. I was thinking of what Annie had said.

When she was young, she said, she lived in the white house, up the hill from my house, above the graveyard.

She was walking one day, when she was young, and all of a sudden there was a man by her side. On the lonely

83

dirt road, in the country, and, all of a sudden, there was someone there.

She told me he was dressed oddly, in a fashion out of the past. And she said she felt frightened.

The man nodded and asked her name. She was young, and had been cautioned by her parents not to talk to strangers, so she didn't respond. He told her that his name was Anders.

She walked up to her farmhouse. Later that night she told her parents. They said that Anders had been the name of the hired man back in their grandparents' time; and it was of this that I was thinking when I walked in the crown of the road by the graveyard that night and something pulled on my coat sleeve.

Then there were the moving stars I'd seen, some fifteen miles from the town, and twenty-five years back.

One winter night, when I was young.

There were five or six of them in the sky. They looked like stars. They would be still for a while. Then they would move and group or cluster for a while, and dart, as if they were chasing one another from one side of the sky to the other.

Sometimes they would shoot across, sometimes they'd move slowly, to the other horizon, where they regrouped into various patterns. I was with several friends. We watched for a while, then telephoned the air-force base in Plattsburgh to report what we'd seen.

The fellow there thanked us. We asked if he had had other reports of the objects, and he said no, he had not. We asked what he thought they might be, and he said he had no idea.

After I got home that night, up my hill, twenty-five years later, once again I saw the lights.

It was four in the morning. I was tired, I was alone in the house. I was brushing my teeth. I glanced out the window, and up the hill, up past the cemetery, past the white house, up the hill, up at the crest of the hill, or as they say, at the height of land, there was a light. It was a bright light, like truck-mounted beacons we would see at a film opening, or like an antiaircraft beacon, scanning the sky. As if it were describing a cone, whose point was on the ground. The shaft of light circled slowly. The beam was much stronger than truck-mounted klieg lights. And it was pure white.

On the ground, beyond the trees at the edge of the field, just at the top of the hill, was this beacon.

I nodded and, in my exhausted state, went on preparing for bed.

And then I asked myself what the light was, up the hill.

"Well, that's just . . ." I started to explain; and then I stopped, as I realized that I had no idea what it was, or what it possibly could be. I set myself to suggest a scenario that would put that light up the hill. I went back to the window, and it still was there, circling slowly.

I was fascinated by the white purity of the light, and I remember thinking that I'd never seen a light that white before. What could it be? It was a signal of some sort, but to whom and by whom?

And why would it be here, in the middle of the night, on a peaceful country road in Vermont?

One summer evening some years back, I had been sitting on the porch of this same house, looking, by chance, up the road at the white house, which was vacant at that time, and I saw a small fire burning below the barn.

I remember that I thought as I watched it, That's just a . . . and, when I could not discount it, I walked up the hill, to find a rapidly spreading fire in the brush, now caught on the barn. I tried to get it out, but it had grown too big for me, so I ran back and called the village fire department.

They got the fire out, and I basked for some long time afterward in a self-awarded sentiment of rural neighborliness.

For, if I had not *seen* it, I thought, or *recognized* it, or investigated it, or acted upon it, the barn and the house would have burned.

And it was the memory of this feeling of neighborliness that moved me to decide to climb the hill to investigate the light.

For there was no one in the white house, and there was no one living in the house beyond it—the house across from the field from which the light was coming.

There was no one on the hill but me; and I must have felt that the light boded malevolence, or danger, for, when I redressed myself and started out of my house, I took a gun.

It was four in the morning of an early spring night as I opened my door, and I congratulated myself on my courage.

Many, I thought, would not venture that half-mile up the hill. Many would stay in their homes, I thought.

And I asked myself why they would do that; and I answered they would do that because the light meant great danger; and I became fearful. I went back in my house, closing the door softly, as one moves when one is a child and moving in the dark so as not to draw the notice of the evil creatures in the room.

I went back in my house, and looked out of the window, and saw the light was still there, up the hill.

I asked myself if I was content to live in ignorance of the nature of the light, and as much as I piqued myself with my cowardice, I found that I wasn't going to climb the hill.

I undressed and got into bed. Although my mind was busy, I fell asleep; and I awakened some time later to a great feeling of fear, and a brilliant, all-pervading white light pouring in my bedroom window, as if the source were down, just outside of my house.

And then I fell asleep again.

The next morning I asked everyone in town if they'd seen or heard anything, or if they could account for the lights I had seen; and they'd seen nothing, and could not explain it.

And down at the bottom of the old sugaring lane on my property, there is a dip in the land at the intersection of the lane with our dirt road which marks the site of the town's earliest settlement two hundred years ago.

In any case, down the hill from my house, the land slopes to a depression at the bottom of what was the old lane. There was and remains something about that spot. I do not like it. I put a small compost pile there. It seemed fitting for a low, hidden, and somehow unpleasant spot.

Perhaps you've noticed spots like that. Not in the city, where the land is covered, but out in the country or the woods.

Perhaps you've felt the spots that are happy, and the spots that exude danger, as if they were sending the message, "Ignore me at your peril. You should not be here."

I put the small compost pile in the hollow at the bottom of the hill.

Up by my house, between the house and the cemetery,

near the road, there was a swing set. And one afternoon I was pushing my daughter on the swing, and my eye went beyond her, down the hill, down to a form by the compost pile. It was the form of a man, and it was dead white, from head to foot.

I saw it for a second, then it disappeared.

I wondered if it had been conjured, somehow, out of my feelings of antipathy for the spot.

Some weeks later, it must have been at the end of summer, for there were apples on the trees, my daughter asked me to climb to get her an apple, which I did.

She took a bite, and told me that it was too early and the apple was sour, and she didn't want any more. "What should I do with it?" she asked, and I told her to walk the fifty feet down to the compost pile.

"No," she said, "I don't want to go there. There's a monster that lives there."

And there were people talking. Outside of various houses in the night. One summer, in a cottage at North Hero; one whole fall, back in the sixties, when I lived with friends in a rented trailer in the woods.

That fall there were two men talking outside all night, night after night, till one of us, left alone one night, called the state police. They searched and found nothing; and when we returned from our school vacations, or wherever we had been, we all said to one another, "Oh, my God, you've heard it, too . . . ?"

Like the old woman at the house outside of Newport.

A friend told me about the house on the lake, and I took it for a summer, and heard the old woman crying and scolding in the night, and went outside so many times to see her, but there was never anything there.

Back in New York in the fall, the friend who'd suggested the house asked how the summer had gone. I told her it went well.

"Is the ghost still there?" she asked.

"Yes," I told her, "the ghost is still there."

Music

I lived two terrible years as a smoker in Cambridge, Massachusetts. Not only was I a smoker, I was a smoker of cigars, and many of them.

I endured the polite signs in places of business and congress, and many impolite reproachful looks and stares of my liberal brethren—those looks that said, "If I were less of a gentleperson, I would be looking at you in such a way as to let you know that your habit, which you must know is unhealthy, but from which you have not the willpower to refrain, is as insulting and offensive to those around you as it is disgraceful to its practitioner."

I became oh-so-tired of wondering whether my cigar smoking was going to elicit the above response, and spent a lot of time thinking about my prospective reply: should I be arrogant and ignore, arrogant and respond, courteous and beg pardon, et cetera.

This, of course, took the thrill out of cigar smoking. My liberal brethren had reduced me to a worried and cowering state on this one issue. I was upbraided in the park for smoking cigars; this park, which, previous to my correction, I had always thought of as "outside." And my last refuge was the lovely tobacco store on Mass Ave, where they let me sit up in the chess gallery and smoke their cigars while I worked—until this previously beloved resort became as a prison to me, and I stopped smoking.

I feel much better since I stopped. My clothes smell clean, my wind and general fitness are improved. I am, as any reformed person, aware of the benefits that this re-form has wrought for the populace in general; and I find that I do object to smoking on planes, in restaurants, and in any place where the nonsmoker has no comfortable means of distance from the offensive object. I think and hope that I neither express nor feel the self-righteousness that I found so dreadful as its recipient, but I do admire the net result of those workers for a smoke-free world—the laws and improvements that they have wrought. It's not something I would have gone to court about, but I'm glad they did.

Now, however, I find it is my ox that is being gored; and though I fear that the quiddity of my objection opens me to ridicule, I am going to state it.

I am offended and upset by the universality of recorded music played in situations where the listener is powerless to escape.

I do not find it necessary that restaurateurs, business-people, and captains of transportation should elect to fill the arguably nonmusical moments in my day with their notion of the correct theme.

I would prefer street sounds, general quiet, or the lovely rhythm of human conversation to music played in a restaurant. Why should the tastes of some restaurant "consultant" predominate over my own predilection for silence?

I prefer the sounds of the gymnasium to the wretched throbbing of disco music, or whatever that phenomenon is called today. I do not like the time I spend weighing the rights of the restaurant against the rights of myself, the customer, each time I try to decide whether to ask that the music be turned off or lowered, or whether I should just leave. I spend a lot of my life in restaurants, on planes. I read in them, I write in them. Both activities are seriously curtailed by the presence of recorded music.

One might argue that said music is simply background, but it is not so for me.

I love music, I play music, I write music, and when it is being played I am unable to tune it out. I am listening to it against my will, distracted from my thoughts, my book, my work, and hating the choice, the fact, and the arrangement, of the music, and the arrogance of those who have subjected me to it. *Can it be* that those of a certain class cannot imbibe their alcohol or chew their food without hearing Ella Fitzgerald or Billie Holiday, that travelers would feel cheated if they did not hear the *Brandenburg Concerto* when the plane touched down, that others could not enjoy their shopping mall without "By the Time I Get to Phoenix"?

I suggest that *no one* enjoys that music. That it is there because it is there, and that most people either do not notice it or have come to accept it as the correct background noise for the above activities.

I can do neither, and, though I know this confession brands me as an old maid, I feel I have a just beef, and you have just heard it.

93

I would not be so quixotic as to suggest that the courts are the proper venue for the settlement of that which even I, the offended, can barely envision as a dispute; but I suspect that there are others of a disposition similar to mine, and that perhaps somewhere we might have some redress.

Those of such mind might be thought of as neurasthenic individuals, but we might also be thought of as consumers—and, in that guise, perhaps we might gain consideration of an entrepreneur or two. If I saw a restaurant advertising "good food, quiet surroundings," I'd surely give it a try.

THE HOTEL LINCOLN

I took down an old acting book the other day.

It was Richard Boleslavsky's *Acting: The First Six Lessons,* and, when I was a young acting student, it was beloved by me. The book was a fairly constant companion in the late sixties and seventies. It is an anecdotal and accessible rendering of Boleslavsky's understanding of that philosophy which, for want of better terminology, should probably be called the Stanislavsky System.

Here is why I took the book down: I was passing in front of my television, which, to my shame, was turned on. The television was advertising an upcoming showing of the film *Lives of a Bengal Lancer.* Well, I thought, I don't know the film, but I love the book. And I strove to prove to the television that my literacy predated the electronic. I scanned the bookcase for the *Lives,* and did not find it. I did, however, come across another book in the, I would think, limited sub-arcana of lancer memoirs, and this book was *Lances Up!*

Now, *Lances Up!* is by Richard Boleslavsky, and describes his career in the Polish Lancers at the beginning of the Great War. I had bought the book during the period when I frequented drama bookstores and because its author had been a member of the Moscow Art Theater—my youthful Camelot—and had written the excellent *Six Lessons*.

So, twenty years later, and involved in a rather pointless dialogue with a television set, my thoughts guided my hand to an old favorite book of mine, and I took it down from the shelf, and a rent receipt fell out of it.

It was a receipt for $170 for one month's rent at the Hotel Lincoln, which stood and stands at the southern end of Lincoln Avenue in Chicago.

I lived at the Lincoln off and on for various years of my youth, and I found it a paradise.

Let me tell you: when I first began staying there the rent was $135 a month, which included daily maid service, an answering service, a television set, and both the best view and the best location in Chicago.

The rooms looked out over Lincoln Park and the lake, and I thought the view much nicer than that afforded by Lake Shore Drive.

I had nothing but Clark Street between me and the park, while Lake Shore Drive had the vast concrete Outer Drive and constant noise and traffic. My room got the most beautiful of sunrises, and it was always clean when I came back at night. I believe I pitied the deluded gentry who paid fortunes for their apartments, and who did not realize that one required nothing more than shelter and solitude. Not only did my hotel room possess those, but it had charm in the bargain. Elaine, the ancient telephone operator, somehow got into the habit of calling me up at eleven or twelve at night and asking if I needed a cup of tea or anything. There was a reported crap game down in the men's room, which I never found; and there was the sound of the animals at night.

The animals lived in the Lincoln Park Zoo, which was pretty much right across the street, and many times at night I'd hear the lions or the seals.

The report of the crap game came from friends at Second City.

As a kid in high school I hung around Second City quite a bit. I was friendly with the owners and their family, and was permitted to frequent the joint. Later I worked there as a busboy, and occasionally I played piano for the kids' shows on the weekend.

In any case, in the early sixties, well before the time of the rent receipt, I was exposed to *la vie bohème* as rendered by the actors at Second City. The club was, at that time, half a block from the Hotel Lincoln restaurant (which was not, I believe, called the Laff-In at that juncture); and it was related to me that various illuminati of the North Side lived in the Hotel Lincoln and ate and wrote and schemed in the hotel restaurant, and shot craps in the men's room, and, having been told these things, I remembered them. And when it became time for me to go out into the world, I applied to the hotel, and was rented a room.

I bought my first typewriter (an Olympia, for which I remember paying two hundred dollars; it seemed like a lot of money for a manual typewriter, but I've still got it, twenty-some years later, and it still works fine) and paid a month in advance and lived at the Hotel Lincoln. I went downstairs several times a day to the restaurant, now called the Laff-In, and sat in the same booths that had once sheltered Burns and Shreiber, Fred Willard, and the great Severn Darden. I received messages at the switchboard, and had beautiful young women back up to my room. I went down to the Laff-In in the middle of the night and had chicken soup with the owner, Jeff, and talked about the world. I never went into the hotel's bar, but did have a drink now and then with the proprietors of the drugstore, behind the prescription counter.

I worked during those years at a day (or "straight") job, and, in one capacity or other, in the theater.

I sold land over the telephone for a while. The real estate office was way up north in Lincolnwood, and so I rode the length of Lincoln Avenue twice each day on the CTA bus, and it seemed significant to me that the long bus route began on the very corner where I lived. (And coming home at night, I could see the red-orange sign of the hotel from as far north, if memory serves, which it probably does not, as Addison Street.)

I worked as a waiter at a club just up Clark Street; and, during that period, I worked as a busboy in the final days of the London House.

I wrote plays in my notebook, sitting in the Laff-In; and wrote sitting on various benches in the park across the street.

I had just a few clothes and several theater books. Looking back, I think that I can say that I not only set out to but managed to emulate a model of the Life of a Chicago Writer.

I had guests at my house in Boston on the evening that I took down the Boleslavsky. One of the guests was a young actor. I started reminiscing with him and his friends about *my* early days in the theater, and told him, as, it seems, we middle-aged fogeys may do, how romantic and how cheap things had been in my day. I told him about the perfect life of charm and comfort lived for $170 a month, and brought out the book and receipt as if the fact of their existence would mitigate my garrulousness. He admired the book, and I made him a present of it, and inscribed it with his name and the wish that it would bring him much enjoyment and luck.

He asked if I meant him to have the receipt too. I hesitated a moment. The receipt had just become precious to me. It was an absolute relic of an earlier day of my life. I wanted the receipt. But what did the receipt signify? That I had, in fact, lived through those times in which I had lived? Who would doubt it, and, equally, to whom could it be important? It could be important only to me, and I knew the truth of it already. So I told the actor that, of course, I meant him to have the receipt, too; because I wanted to be part of the succession through Boleslavsky to Stanislavsky and the Moscow Art Theater, and I was flattered that the young man wanted to make the tradition continue to himself through me.

THE SHOOTING
AUCTION

I took the train out of Union Station in Chicago, and went south. I was going to meet a man I had known only over the phone. He ran an auction house for firearms. I'd bought several pieces from him, and sold a piece or two as well.

The last auction had in it a .45-caliber Colt pistol of mine. I'd had the gun extensively reworked and tuned for shooting competition. But business had taken me away from practice, so I decided to clean out my gun cabinet and sent it down to the auction house.

The pistol and the modifications had run me well over a thousand dollars, but the auction was a place to find a bargain; I would be lucky to get eight hundred for the gun.

After the auction the proprietor phoned and told me that he was extremely sorry, but that my gun had only fetched $275. He was surprised and apologetic, and offered to waive his commission, but I told him, no, that I'd profited as a buyer at the auction, and that I knew the rules of the game, and that the pistol had fetched what the market thought it was worth, that he should deduct his commission and send me a check.

He then invited me down to his place in southern Illinois to see the operation, pick up the check, and do a little shooting at his range.

I was flattered by the invitation, which was, I knew, offered partly by way of apology for what he considered my disappointment at the auction price. I am not a gregarious person, and, further, wouldn't have wanted the man to feel beholden to me; but my experience of the shooting sports was of an exceedingly friendly and hospitable fraternity. My acquaintance with the owner of the auction had grown over the time of our business dealings. He seemed a friendly man, and his invitation to come down south and do a little shooting was very much in the fairly universally, in my experience, friendly style of the shooting world. His offer caught me in between projects, and a trip and some shooting sounded like a very good idea, so I got on the train and rode south.

He and his friend met me at the station, and we went to his friend's house. The man had a large collection of American shotguns. There were perhaps eighty of them displayed horizontally on every wall of his gun room. On a table in the center of the room was a scale-model steamboat he had made. The damn thing was about two feet end to end and fashioned completely out of brass. I was told that it was detail-correct down to the smallest fittings and gauges and that it operated perfectly.

This seemed a bit obsessive, and I found myself repressing an impulse to question the infinite completion of the model. "But surely," I wanted to say, "it can't have *every* gauge and fitting of the original . . ." But I held my tongue, although I found the intricacy of the model aggressive, and I admired his collection of arms.

One of his prizes was a German drilling, a double shotgun with a rifle barrel underneath. The guns are, I understand, popular in Europe, but I had never seen one. And its oddity was accentuated by various features fitted into the stock that would change the point-of-aim when the shooter changed from shotgun to rifle. The drilling had a comb-and-cheek piece that popped out of the stock when a button was pushed, and it was very well made and very German and I admired it no end.

The door to the friend's gun room was taken from a bank vault. Walking in his hallway, one opened a door to what could have been a linen closet, and found, beyond it, the massive steel vault door.

The two men gathered and advertised their guns each month in an old-fashioned hand-drawn brochure. I collected the brochures and bid on a few of the guns, and I sent some in to be sold, including, as I've said, the Colt .45 automatic.

The two men were to drive me out to their club. We went south through very flat farm country, over the blacktop road. In a while the land became slightly rolling and more wooded. We went off on a side road and then through a stretch of woods to the shooting club.

The club, I was told, was a rather exclusive affair and drew membership from all over the Midwest. Admittance had been closed for some long time, and new membership opportunities tended to devolve almost exclusively upon the family and friends of the old members.

Additionally, to apply, one must have spent, I was told, ninety days "under canvas." I had never heard the

expression before, and thought it somewhat overly picturesque, until I reflected that my reluctance to embrace it
was probably founded on both envy and ignorance of the
situation it described; and to the world that would have
need to refer to the phenomenon, the phrase was not only
apt, but, to the contrary of my suspicions of its pretti-
ness, direct and businesslike in the extreme.

As we drove through the club's long driveway—we
have all, I think, had that experience of first exposure to
a secluded and exclusive spot, in which the drive from the
barred gate to the main buildings seems interminable—I
was pointed out the house of the gamekeeper.

We drove past it, and over the various streams and past
the small lake of the shooting-club preserve. I was told
the names of the streams and how the ice fishing took
place and the ponds were stocked, and how the wives of
the sportsmen prepared this or that traditional dinner on
its appointed date.

We drove to a small cabin and parked. The cabin was
furnished with a few long tables and a wooden chair or
two. Around the walls were lockers and shelving.

My companions signed into a log book and took some
targets from a bin, and we went outside, out beyond the
cabin, where there was a hundred-yard rifle range.

The owner's friend took the targets and walked the
hundred yards down to the butts. The owner and I went
back around to the car and opened the trunk and took out
several rifles, ear protectors, and a canvas shooting bag.

We took the lot over to a shooting table back at the
firing line, and laid out the rifles, side by side. The man
took a sandbag from the shooting gear and pointed to one
of the rifles and asked me if I'd go first.

We saw the other man hoist up the targets, down at the end of the range. I waited, with that schematic shooting courtesy which always has in it just that little bit of "show," for him to return and move well back of the firing line before I prepared to shoot.

The rifle was some very quick and flat-shooting thing. A 220 Swift or something. A varmint rifle. I took the sandbag, whacked it down on the table in front of me, and pounded a valley into it with the edge of my hand. I opened the bolt of the rifle and laid the stock in the sandbag groove. The man gave me five rounds of ammunition, and I took them and put them next to the sandbag. I sat down in the metal chair and pulled it up to the shooting table.

I asked him if it was all right to dry-fire the piece and he said it was. I got down behind the rifle and looked through the scope. The eye relief was good for me, and it brought the target right up close. I got myself into a good shooting position, my left arm across my chest and the hand hugging the right shoulder; I closed the bolt and took aim at the target. I took a deep breath. In and slowly out; then in and half out, until the crosshairs rested exactly on the bottom center of the bull's-eye, and I squeezed the trigger, which broke clean at what felt like around three and a half pounds. I opened the bolt, looked up from the rifle, and loaded the five rounds down into the magazine. "Well, I guess I'm going to shoot here," I said. The two men nodded and stepped farther back from the firing line.

I put four shots into the target, and they felt so good that I got a bit nervous and pulled the fifth shot slightly. "Flyer!" I called out after the last shot, and immediately felt foolish, as if anything in the world depended upon the consistency of my shooting.

I opened the bolt, and one of the men said I had shot very well. But I couldn't get over my last shot, and compounded my feelings of gaucherie by going on about it. "No," I said. "Last shot's way off. Way off."

We walked down to the butts and pulled the target down, and it showed four shots in a one-inch group just right of center at the bottom of the bull, and the fifth shot three quarters of an inch below and to the right of the group.

This was good shooting, even with the flyer, and both honesty—I was shooting rather above my head—and courtesy required that I shut up about it and let the next man shoot. But I just couldn't seem to keep quiet, and I kept going on about how the rifle "felt," and what a good rifle it was, and how I had pulled the last shot. I felt like a fool and knew that my chat sounded false to the other men.

We put up some fresh targets and went back to the firing line, and shot some of the other rifles, but I was all over the target and couldn't get any of them to group.

I told the men I had to catch a 4 P.M. train back to Chicago. They asked me to stay on and shoot more, but I said I had to go.

We drove back through the farm country, into the town, and to the auction house. The owner showed me around his operation—how the good pieces were separated from the lesser ones, how they were all cleaned and logged and photographed. I walked through the aisles and looked at the various items in the bins.

It was about time to leave for the station. We were

back in his office, drinking coffee and making our fare-wells. I admired a good-looking pistol in a box on a shelf.

"That one's mine," the owner said. "Picked up for a song. I stole it for two hundred fifty dollars."

I picked up the pistol to admire it, and saw it was the one I'd sent him to be sold.

WABASH AVENUE

Wabash Avenue ran under the El.

The significant part was eight blocks long. It ran from Randolph Street on the north to Van Buren on the south.

Wabash was the backside of Michigan Avenue.

Michigan was show. Fronted on the park, it looked out on statuary, the Art Institute, and the lake. It was a grand white-stone European vision. Michigan Avenue was old Chicago money patting itself on the back.

Wabash, running parallel, was, to me, a truer Chicago. The street was always dark. It ran underneath the El; the sun never hit Wabash Avenue. It was always noisy. It was a masculine street. It was a business street. As a kid I'd hang out on the fourth floor of Marshall Field's store for men on Wabash and Washington. That was a store for a young kid to be in.

The fourth floor had a Kodiak bear to greet you as you got off the elevator. The bear had been shot by one of the customers and donated to the store; and I always wondered what kind of man would shoot such a bear and then keep it anywhere other than in his living room. I still wonder.

In any case, it was on its hind legs and *looming* over you as you got off. Ten, twelve feet in the air. There were other animals and heads and fish displayed throughout the floor, but the bear was *it* in my book.

Over on the right was the gun section. You had to pass through the fishing rods to get to them, but it was a short walk.

Over on the left they kept the clothing. I don't remember much about the clothing on the fourth floor. I remember the hats on two.

My usual rounds took me from the fourth floor down the stairs to two. They had the most magnificent assortment of hats I have ever seen in my life.

Every summer I would try on countless straw boaters before deciding that neither the times nor my personality would support my sporting one. One summer I actually bought one, but I don't remember wearing it.

I also remember buying a beret or two over the years from the second floor. Very romantic. Not the $150 extra-select Panamas—a true fortune in the early sixties; not the sable or marten trappers' hats, so beautiful I didn't even feel fit to ask to try them on; no, I bought a beret once or twice over the years, and wore it out of the store, feeling myself the creditable and up-to-the-minute rendition of a serious young man with artistic aspirations.

The ground floor of the store was haberdashery. I have looked that word up many times over the years, as every time I see it I am puzzled by its derivation. I am going to look it up once again. I see my dictionary tells me it comes from the Middle English, *haberdassherie,* and it becomes clear to me I need a new or auxiliary dictionary.

In any case, I always felt the word was silly. Further, it was associated in my mind, of course, with Harry Truman, a man whom I did not associate with relaxed elegance. Neither endowment, however, lessened my affection for the first floor, which was the Hermès and Charvet's of Chicago. Man, they had a fine line of goods in there—their like may still exist, but I haven't seen it.

I remember the most beautiful shirts and socks and underwear and belts and suspenders and leather goods. Truman Capote had said it of Tiffany's; "Nothing very bad could happen to you there."

The store was always deliciously cool in the summertime, and warm in the winter, on those very cold and very dark nights, when you would have to go out of that haven and fight your way through the people on Wabash who were trying to fight their way through you and get home just like you. And the lucky ones were going on the El, where at least they had a bit of shelter, and you were usually going on the bus, and had to stand on Washington Street, exposed to that cold, which is worse than any I've ever felt anywhere else.

And what is there about the El? I don't know. I notice that in almost every thriller made in Chicago in the last few years, there is a chase sequence involving the El, and someone riding on top of the El. Well, the El is, of course, romantic, but why would anyone want to ride on top? I always loved it, as it took you out of the cold. I never lived near the El, and always wished that I did.

I remember the El outside the practice studios at Lyon and Healy's. I used to while away many hours at the rate, if memory serves, of one dollar per, in the small piano rooms there. I always requested one on the Wabash side, facing the El. That was my Tin Pan Alley—just me and a pack of cigarettes, playing the piano in the closet-sized room . . . the El thundering by outside the fourth-floor window.

They were great people at Lyon and Healy's. In fact, as I think about it, I don't remember any salespeople on Wabash who were other than great to me. I spent untold hours in the shops, fingering the stuff, questioning the clerks, making only the most minimal purchases, and those rarely. They let me play all the guitars at Lyon and Healy's, and across the street at Prager and Ritter's.

The salespeople at Abercrombie and Fitch told me about all the custom knives in the first-floor cases. The first major sporting purchase of my life was made there. After much deliberation, and after much saving, I bought a Randall #5 bird-and-trout knife out of the case at Abercrombie's.

It cost fifty-five dollars. It was, and still is, advertised as the knife that Francis Gary Powers was carrying when his U2 was shot down over Russia. I don't know why, but that seemed, and still rather seems, a legitimate endorsement. I suppose that was what Wabash Avenue was to me—a very romantic street. It had the weight of seriously romantic endeavors—hunting, music, dress, reading. I got my first credit card from Kroch's and Brentano's bookstore. I was, I believe, seventeen years old, and they gave me a credit card.

I discovered literature in their basement paperback section. I discovered contemporary writing on the first floor. The salespeople would order books for me, then would look the other way while I stood at the rack and read that week's new book. I felt like a member there.

What a different world. I remember the salesmen at Iwan Ries tobacco store schooling me in the niceties of tobacco smoking as they sold me my first pipe—delighted to be passing on a tradition. I remember buying English Oval cigarettes there. I loved the box and the shape. Someone told me that you were supposed to squeeze them to recompress them into a round shape, but I never did this, and if it was the right thing to do, I didn't want to know. They tasted, to me, of powder and the very exotic—much more so than the heavier Balkan Sobranies, which, it must be admitted, came in the best package anything has ever come in—that small, flat white metal tin, which held ten cigarettes; or, later, a couple of bills and a driver's license, vitamins—it occurs to me that, even at the time, one knew that there were not really a hell of a lot of things that the Sobranie case was perfectly suited to accommodate—but what promise it offered.

That was Wabash Avenue. They were glad to see you smoke, glad to see you enjoy yourself, glad to help you do it, and delighted that they could earn their living by assisting you. I suppose it was the end of Chicago as the Merchant to the Frontier.

What am I forgetting? Up at the top, at Wacker, is the statuary group of General Washington, and somebody else, and significantly, to me, a Mr. Solomon—if memory serves—who is there inscribed as a merchant supporter of the Continental Cause. Away down the other end of Wabash were the main garages and offices of the Yellow Cab Company, where I had one or two interesting encounters during my days as a cabdriver, but the *real* Wabash ran just for those eight or nine blocks under the El.

Various Sports in Sight of the Highlands

I try to pop over to Scotland for a little golf once every forty-three years.

As there exists both religious theory and folk belief to the effect that, should one scorn someone or something in this life, in the life to come one will *become* that thing; so, in my introduction to golf, did I reap what I had sown.

For I had spent some time—as who could escape it—watching folks devoted to golf in that same way and with that same devotion others give to cats or the First Amendment, or to other sports and articles capable both of use and of receiving devotional fervor.

I had watched these folks and wondered. As a child, I spent far too much time in a new suburb of Chicago, which suburb's only claim to fame was that it bordered a golf course of, I believe, national distinction. And one summer, some *première-classe* golf contest was held there and neighbors of mine made a lot of money renting out space in a cornfield to those who had come to watch the golf.

And I had, of course, putted through the windmill, and

into the mouth of the gorilla at those carny spots named "Putt 'n' Grin," and so on, on too-hot midwestern evenings.

As to golf itself, however, I was as innocent as the babe unborn is held to be under some of the more lenient of religious persuasions; and I had come to Scotland to learn.

I approached my first lesson with this attitude: how craven it would be to wish to excel at a sport the clothing of whose participants I had laughed at for so many years. And, as it turned out, I was not in any danger at all of so excelling.

I was welcomed at a beautiful resort devoted to sport, and put into the care of an excellent teacher, who showed me the position of the feet, of the hands, of the head and knees, and of the shoulders. I was shown how to relax the shoulders through raising the chin; and how the angle of the ball was sure to depend on the position of the club as it came to the ball, and how that was assured of depending on the angle of the backswing.

My excellent teacher broke it down section by section, and I was sweating with the effort of it all after a few minutes.

It reminded me hugely of the hook. My boxing coach said, of that other worthy mystery, "Yeah, you try and try, and one day, next week, next month, *sometime,* one day, 'Dawn over Marble Head.' " Well, in time the hook began to make sense; and I, as I say, see the similarity in the golf swing.

In both, it seems to me, the hands and arms are along for the ride, and the legs and waist are doing the yeoman work; so the acquisition of both the hook and the golf swing must be a process of breaking it down, and learning the components by rote over lengthy periods during which one has nothing better to do.

This whole idea was fine with me, but I had been allotted only two half-hour lessons with the instructor, after which I was to play nine rounds with the resort's golf pro. At the end of my first half hour I had only progressed as far as missing the ball completely whilst concentrating on the movements of my arms and torso; and my second and last bout of tuition boded fair to consist of missing the ball while employing my entire frame.

Well, I consoled myself, what is golf anyway?

Nothing, I reflected, short of some bastard amalgam of billiards and hiking.

It was, I said in my fit of pique, guilty of falling into that category of most despicable of activities, something that would "ruin the drape." My preferred leisure hours of the last forty years have consisted of playing the piano or playing poker, a signal desideratum consonant to the two that they do not ruin the drape.

In neither the playing of the piano nor the playing of cards do we find the necessity of carrying around weighty, bulky, or awkward objects that would deform the clean and flowing lines of the nifty clothing elected by nature as appropriate to the pursuit of such endeavors. One cannot say the same of golf.

Yes, I understand that one is theoretically empowered to subdue the energy of human or mechanical caddies to carry one's golf clubs, but this seems to me an unattractive alternative for two reasons.

First, I think that there must be those times when one must carry the clubs some small way—even if that way is as limited as from the baggage carousel to the car—and this would ruin the drape.

Yes, you might say, but could one not simply point the golf clubs out to a porter and have him or her carry them that offending distance?

Yes, I reply, one could; but this would put one afoul of that which I feel is the second serious disqualification of the sport: it seems to me that a whole big bunch of time and space has to be put aside to play golf.

My hero, Thorstein Veblen, wrote in *The Theory of the Leisure Class* that the lawn, as we know it, is nothing more or less than the attempt to re-create a field that has been munched down by sheep—thus conferring upon its owners the status of gentlemen and -women farmers. Well, when I got up to Scotland, his point was driven home. My approach to the resort was through a vale called Glen Devon.

The car left Edinburgh and climbed higher and higher through green fields and country lanes until the land fell away on the left side and there was one of the most magnificent views it has ever been my pleasure to see.

I saw a steep mountain valley and, climbing away up the far side, sheep dotted on the hill, untold miles of intersecting stone walls, grass grazed down to look like the finest and most cared-for lawn, which had, on scant reflecting, and with homage to Mr. Veblen, been mowed down to resemble this vale.

And I looked out at the golf course, on which such obvious and loving care had been expended; and, to my untutored eye, it looked identical to the sheep-shorn little hills beyond it. But it was Coco Chanel, I think, who said that there are two good reasons to buy anything, because it is very cheap or because it is very expensive.

And I thought that, for myself, an indulgence in golf spoke too much of what Mr. Veblen called "conspicuous consumption," of both land and energy.

Now, I am no one to talk, for I am sure that I defy all but the most hardened and deluded golfers to have spent more on their clubs than I have spent flogging an obviously beaten pair of eights. And I am proud to have spent that most precious of commodities, my youth, mured in an area that, human nature being what it is, I have come to identify as the esthetically correct venue for sport: a small and smoky room.

So, go in peace, you golfers. Go your way and I will go mine. I returned for that lesson which was to unify in sport the higher and lower portions of my body, and, I think, learned a thing or two, and, I must say, looked forward to my meeting with the golf pro and our round of golf.

But it was raining hard that day, and the pro and I never got to play.

I spent a most pleasant half hour sitting with him in his office. I asked him about the birds I had seen on the golf course, and if, in his experience, they ever came to grief.

He told me that over the years he had knocked down a bird or two, and that, in his youth, he had even taken the odd one back home and cooked it.

He explained that a golf ball can be moving at upward of 120 miles an hour, and that these things happen. He told me that once, in fact, he downed a sheep.

Well, that was good enough for me. I unbuttoned my coat and relaxed, and we had a real good chat about sport, and hustling, and betting, and what a fine world it was to allow one to make a living doing what one loved.

I could have spent the day there, but he was a man with

work to do, so I excused myself, and thanked him for his time, and moved on.

The rain continued to come down and the resort liaison asked if I would like to essay one of the other activities in the tuition and the practice of which they are famed.

I acceded and went in the rain to their shooting school, where, under the tutelage of another excellent instructor, I delighted in breaking several clay pigeons, and returned after a while, wet and cold and glowing, to the shooting lodge, looking for a short drink of Scotch and feeling like a real sporting gent.

The rain was letting up a wee bit, and the golfers were preparing to play. Not my sport, as I have pointed out, but the people who pursue it certainly are serious, and as I looked at them teeing up in the rain I reflected that any leisure endeavor which can be pursued to the point of monomania is worthy of respect, and I was warmed by both the Scotch and my own generosity.

MY HOUSE

In my younger days in New York everyone I knew lived in a walk-up apartment building, and I didn't know anyone who lived below the fifth floor.

At least that is the way my memory has colored it.

I remember the industrial wire spools that served as coffee tables, and the stolen bricks and boards out of which everyone constructed bookcases. There were red-and-yellow Indian bedspreads on the wall, and everyone had Milton Glaser's poster of a Medusa–haired Bob Dylan displayed.

That was how the counterculture looked in Greenwich Village in the sixties. We considered ourselves evolved beyond the need for material comfort, and looked back on a previous generation's candle-in-the-Chianti bottle as laughable affectation.

We children of the middle class were playing proletariat, and, in the process, teaching ourselves the rules of that most bourgeois of games: the Decoration of Houses.

The game, as we learned it, was scored on cost, provenance, integrity of the scheme, and class loyalty.

Now, in those days, status was awarded to the least costly article, and, as for provenance, those articles that were stolen ranked highest, followed immediately by those that had been discarded, with those that had been merely borrowed ranking a weak third.

Objects were capable of being included in the *ensemble* if they were the result of or made reference to the Struggle for a Better World; and points were given to the more geographically or politically esoteric items.

I look around my living room today and see that, of course, none of the rules have changed. They stand just as Thorstein Veblen described them a hundred years ago. The wish for comfort and the display of status contend with and inform each other in the decoration of the living place, and I'm still pretending.

Now, however, I am faking a long-term membership in a different class.

I live in an old row house in Boston.

The house is in an area called the South End, specifically in that section called the Eight Streets. These streets are lined with near-identical bow-front brick row houses, built in the 1870s as part of a housing development and intended as single-family residences. The panic of 1873 wounded the real estate market, and the row houses were, in the main, partitioned and rented out by the room.

My house, the local historical association tells me, is one of the few that were not partitioned. Consequently, it retains most of the architectural detail with which it was adorned a hundred and some years ago. It has beautiful mahogany banisters and intricate newel posts, the stairwell and the rooms on the parlor floor have ornate plaster molding, there are pocket doors with etched glass—the house was built with new mass-construction techniques that enabled the newly bourgeois to suggest to themselves that they were living like the rich.

I bought the house and thought to enjoy the benefits of restoring it to a Victorian grandeur that it most probably never enjoyed. I recalled the lessons of the sixties, and obtained the services of a decorator, who, in this case, was not a security-lax construction company, but a very talented Englishwoman named Susan Reddick.

Now, if fashion is an attempt by the middle class to co-opt tragedy, home decor is a claim to history.

I grew up on the South Side of Chicago, surrounded by sofas wrapped in thick clear plastic. My parents and the parents of all my friends were the children of immigrants, and they started their American dream homes with no artifacts and without a clue, so, naturally, that history to which I laid claim was late-Victorian Arts and Crafts.

That is the era which I am pretending bore and endorsed me—a time which was genteel yet earthy, Victorian in its respect for the proprieties, yet linked through its respect for craft to the eternal household requirement for utility and the expression of that truth in pottery and textiles. What a crock, eh?

But that is whom I am pretending to be, a latter-day William Morris, who suggested that a man should be able to compose an epic poem and weave a tapestry at the same time.

And that is the fantasy which my house probably expresses.

There are a lot of fabrics woven on a hand loom by a neighbor in Vermont, some nice examples of American art pottery, and rooms painted in various unusual colors, and applied with several arcane techniques of stippling, striation, and what may, or at least should, be called dappling.

My wife and I are very comfortable here. We spend a lot of time lounging on overstuffed furniture and reading or writing or talking in our own two-person Bloomsbury salon.

It is, as we would have said in Chicago, a real nice house.

SEVENTY-FIRST AND JEFFERY

The area from Seventy-first Street north to the park was, in my youth, a Jewish neighborhood.

My grandmother took me shopping and spoke in what could have been Yiddish, Polish, or Russian to several of the shopkeepers on Seventy-first Street. She even knew one or two of them from the Old Country, which was the town of Hrubieszów, on the Russian-Polish border. We lived on Euclid Avenue in a brick house.

There was a policeman, or guard, hired by some sort of block or neighborhood association, and his name was Tex. He patrolled the street with two stag-handled revolvers on his belt, one worn butt forward and the other worn butt to the rear. He would stop and chat at length with us kids.

We spent as much time as possible out in the street. The manhole covers did duty as second base and home plate, or the two end zones, as the season demanded.

We would stay out far past dark in the summertime chasing one another around the neighborhood in what we called a "bike chase," which, if memory serves, was some version of the war game the New Yorkers called "ringalevio."

We went looking for lost golf balls at the city's Jackson Park course, four blocks to the north; and would trek in the park all the way over to the lake, where we'd look over at the South Shore Country Club.

The country club was, our parents told us, restricted, which meant closed to Jews. It was more a mysterious than a disturbing landmark. It held down the southeastern corner of my world.

Coming back west down Seventy-first Street, we passed the Shoreland Delicatessen, and the next oasis following was J. Leslie Rosenblum, "Every Inch a Drugstore."

Rosenblum's was, to me, a place from a different world. I found the style of the name foreign and distinctly un-Jewish in spite of the surname. The store itself was, if I may, the Apollonian counterbalance to the Ashkenazic Dionysia of the Shoreland. Rosenblum's was close and somewhat dark and quiet.

Its claim to my attention was a soda fountain, which smelled of chocolate and various syrups and that indefinable rich coolness coming off the marble, which, I fear, must remain unknown to subsequent generations. My dad took me there for Chicago's famous chocolate phosphate.

I would like to conclude the gastronomic tour of South Shore with mention of the Francheezie. That *ne plus ultra* of comestibles was the product of the Peter Pan restaurant, then situated on the corner of Seventy-first and Jeffery Boulevard, the crossroads of South Shore. The Francheezie was a hot dog split down the middle, filled with cheese, and wrapped in bacon, and, to be round, it was good.

The other spots of note to my young mind were the two movie theaters, the Hamilton to the east and the Jeffery to the west of Jeffery Boulevard. The latter was a block and a half from my house.

On Saturdays I'd take my quarter and get over to the movie house. The cartoons started, I believe, at 9 A.M., and there were so many of them. The figure I remember is "100 cartoons."

At seven minutes per, I calculate that they would occupy almost twelve hours, and that can't be right; but I prefer my memory to my reason. In any case, there were sufficient cartoons to keep the kids in the movie theater until past dark on Saturday, and that was where we stayed.

The Jeffery and the Hamilton both boasted large blue dimly lit domes set into their ceilings, and my young mind would many times try to reason what their use might be. I found them slightly Arabic, and forty years later, can almost recall the fantasies I had gazing at them. I believe one of the domes had stars, and the other did not.

We had lemonade stands in the summer, and we trick-or-treated in the fall to the smell of the leaves burning in everyone's yard.

I remember fistfights at Parkside School, and the smell of blood in my nose as I got beaten up by the friend of a friend, for some remark I'd made for which I think I deserved to get beaten up.

Years later, I lived up on the North Side.

I drove a yellow cab out of Unit 13, on Belmont and

Halsted, and I got a fare to a deserted area, where I got a knife put to my throat and my receipts stolen.

The fellow took the money and ran off. I lit a cigarette and sat in the cab for a while, then drove off to look for a cop. I told the cop what had happened, and suggested that if he wanted to pursue the robber, I would come and help him, as the man couldn't be too far away.

He nodded and started taking down information. I told him my name, and he asked if I was related to the people who used to live in South Shore; and it turned out he'd bought our house. We talked about the house for a while, and what it had been like, and how it had changed; and we both agreed that the robber would be long gone.

I drove off in the cab, and that was my last connection with the old neighborhood.

CANNES

Somebody told me this story. It was, he said, the quint-essential experience of Cannes. He went the year Paul Schrader brought his film *Mishima,* and as part of some presentation, an actor on the stage, dressed in a kimono, knelt and went through the motions of ritual suicide. As the audience filed from the auditorium, they were greeted by a double row of eight-foot-high Care Bears passing out candy and leaflets advertising *Care Bears Movie II.*

Similarly, in my own story, there I was in the Grand Hôtel du Cap, surely the most beautiful hostelry on earth. We were having a celebratory lunch following the open-ing of our movie *Homicide.* Many members of the U.S. press were invited to the hotel by Ed Pressman, one of the film's producers. Ed stood and made a toast. He pointed out that it was perhaps something more than ironic that we were celebrating the premiere of a movie by Jews and about Jews in the building that had housed the Nazi headquarters for the Riviera during World War II.

Is this more or less ironic than the Care Bears? After three days in Cannes I cannot tell.

After a sleepy arrival at the Nice airport, my fiancée, Miss Pidgeon, and I are gradually whisked to the Carlton Hotel, said transport's progress attenuated by the ministrations of a well-meaning group I could only take to be the festival's officialdom, who met us at the airport and insisted on our transportation in state, which insistence would have been rather more appreciated if they could have found the car, but there's a price for everything.

We got to what probably isn't referred to as "downtown Cannes" and there was the Carlton, a grand Victorian, foursquare edifice that would have looked right at home in Brighton, save for two things: it was in actual good repair, and it was tarted-out road to roof with billboards advertising films and stars, most of which no one had ever heard of. So in we go. Someone informs me that the thing to have is a suite on the sea side. I ask for a suite on the sea side, and am informed that they have been booked years in advance, and that I should only live so long and prosper as the time in which I am not going to have a suite on the sea side. So we go up to the room and go to sleep, and then it is the next day.

I decide to break a several-years'-long avoidance of coffee, so I have one cup and then another and then several more, and we go out onto the beach to have a good time.

I have been informed that bare-breasted women walk the beach at Cannes, their favorite pet a leashed pig. (I tell the story to a Vietnam-veteran friend of mine on my return and he says, "Oh. Those potbellied Asian pigs. We used to shoot 'em for sport. I should have brought them back under my shirt—I hear they fetch a thousand dollars.") But I saw no pigs. I did see the bare-breasted women, and it all seemed quite civilized to me. Also I saw many people walking dogs. Many had French poodles, which seemed a bit "on the nose," but what are you going to do?

I also saw a lot of the kind of off-brand mutts that appear only in dog books and paintings of Italian royalty, and I saw women of a certain age bringing their dogs to work. The dogs ranged in size downward from the small-medium to the ludicrous category. I saw one dog that was of a breed so small that I think the owner explained to me that she had to have two of them, as one was not large enough to hold all the organs. But my French is by no means perfect, and it is possible I misunderstood.

Dawned the next day, Wednesday, and Miss Pidgeon and I repaired to the beach, I say, there to sit and bask away our jet lag.

She was garbed in a classic one-piece maillot, and I had on jeans and a T-shirt, hoping to hide the physique I had worked so assiduously to acquire all winter.

Next to us was a French couple. I engaged them in conversation, and they told me they adored film, that their lucky number was eight, and that they had come down to Cannes when they heard that this was the forty-fourth film festival, said digits being combinable into eight, and here they were.

He was in the fur and leather business, and he told me that fur had had it, and that he feared that leather wasn't very far behind. I asked him if this was because of a certain growing sympathy for animals, and he said that a conjunction of that regrettable development and the inscrutable wave motion of fashion had "put paid" to his life's work, but that he was branching out into fibers, and that I shouldn't worry.

"Why is it," I asked, "that, *ici-bas,* we give our fullest sympathy to them little rodents out of whom we make the furs, but are not so vehemently inclined toward their bovine brethren from whom we fashion the hides?" And well may you believe that that drained to oblivion the high school French to which I wasn't even paying attention thirty years ago. In response to my query, he shrugged. He shrugged and I nodded sagely, and no one has ever felt more Continental than I did at that instant. We spent the day on the beach, and lunched at the Terrace Café there, and listened to the peddlers hawking sunglasses and various pornographic materials, and had a fine old time all day.

Down went the sun. The film producers arrived and we all walked to the Festival Hall to do a sound check on the movie.

We walked down the Croisette, which I believe is the name of the main beach. The producers bought ice cream cones. Out in the harbor were several billionaires' yachts. All of us wondered if such people could be happy, and individually decided that they could not, and felt very pleased with ourselves.

We got to the hall, and after a predictable runaround looking for the right person to accept our credentials, we were admitted. Now, this hall seats around twenty-five hundred people, I think. It is vast. There is no end to it. Each of its dimensions is larger than all the others combined. I am introduced to various officials of the festival, and to the representative of Dolby Sound. I have never understood what the Dolby process does, but I am sure it is something important. The film's producers tell me that we have to stay only for a few minutes, to make sure that "things" are in order. I nod. The festival functionaries chat among themselves, and the fellow sitting next to me explains that I have a direct line to the projectionist should I want to communicate anything to him. I rack my brain. What, I think, might I conceivably want to say to the projectionist? I am capable of remembering that the film might be out of focus, and there my mind stops. I also cannot remember the French for "focus," which is, given the damnable unpredictability of their corrupt tongue, most likely "focus."

So I sit there holding the phone, while various preparations are made for the screening.

The producers and the Dolby man have stopped chatting. Evidently *un ange passé*. I decide to fill the gap. "What's the throw?" I say. This is the one question I know how to ask about an actual movie theater. The *throw* is the distance from the projector to the screen, and what it affects, and what throw is desirable, I could not tell you with a gun to my head. So I do not listen too closely to the response, the lights go out, and the film begins.

There are about ten of us in this hall built for twenty-five hundred. The film is preceded by two rather garish video logos for companies that, I think, coughed up part of the European money to finance the project. The festival functionary asks me if I want the logos in or out. I confer with my producers. They say to leave it in as a mark of respect. So be it.

The film looks great, but I can't hear a word of it. There are hurried conversations. It turns out that the stereo recording is on the widest speakers, and that the hall is so big we are getting an echo effect. The sound is then switched onto the middle two speakers, and it sounds a bit better.

I think the film looks dark. I ask the functionary and he tells me some technical info about how a film has to look darker on a screen that big, because if the projector lamps were turned up higher, something or other would happen. "Well, if *that's* the case," I tell him, "*fine.*" I'm supposed to watch only a few minutes of the film. But I have invited my Parisian friends from the beach, and I do not want to disappoint them, so we all stay through the whole film.

The film is over. I expect the festival people to be weeping copiously or ritually rending their garments or something by way of encouragement; but my hopes, it seems, are too high, and they shake my hand and say they enjoyed the film and wish me well.

We all walk back along the Croisette. There are many people out walking around and looking in the windows of the very posh shops. Many of the people have dogs.

The drivers speed viciously. The hotel room has no air-conditioning. These are my reflections as I fall into a jet-lagged sleep. When I awake it has become Thursday, the day of the opening of the festival, which festival will be opened by the screening of my film.

My schedule for Thursday looked like this: interviews in the morning, then a trip to the Festival Hall for a press conference and a session with photographers, then more interviews, then the official festival opening screening, and then a party given by Jack Lang, the cultural minister of France. A full day.

I looked forward to doing all of my interviews on the

beach, but when I awoke, it was pissing down rain, and so it was going to be interviews in the hotel room.

I said a prayer that I wouldn't make a fool of myself during my meetings with the press. I hadn't done any interviews for the last several years, and felt much better for it.

When I stopped talking to the press, I began to see the publicity process from an interesting remove—a bit like the fellow who has turned teetotal, and goes to the cocktail party and wonders why everyone is behaving in such an odd fashion and what they find so amusing in one another.

The publicity process had come to seem to me a good example of jolly mutual exploitation, and not unlike my memories of the climate of sexual promiscuity in the turbulent sixties—something that also seemed a good idea at the time.

In the publicity process the subject and the interlocutor both pretend to be disinterested. The interviewee is constrained to adopt some version of a humble demeanor ("Who *me* . . . ?"), and the interviewer poses as an honest seeker after truth—either for his own edification or on behalf of his readership.

In truth, the subject is trying to flog his wares, his ideas, or himself, and the journalist is—usually—hoping to "catch him out," as it "makes better copy." And I can't say that I blame the journalist. Which, if we're looking for a villain, leaves the subject, which, in my case, was myself, which is why I stopped doing interviews. For it did seem to me to be two overweening ids—the Chorus Girl and the Producer; and the Chorus Girl said, "I am going to bed with you because I am taken with your kindness and your generosity—two qualities I find attractive in a man"; and the Producer said, "I respect your honesty and your integrity in going to bed with a man old enough to be your uncle, and, further, I am impressed with your fortitude in withstanding the sure-to-come barbs of those deluded souls who might say that you are going to bed with me just to get the part, and, in *spite* of them, I am going to give you the part, which I was going to do anyway."

And then we have the superego of the Bellhop, who says, "Oh, *please*. . . . Whyn't'cha just hop in the sack and get *on* with it."

So I said a prayer that I would not make a fool of myself, and reminded myself of the supposed benefits of publicity, and went forth. I talked to a couple of journalists in the morning and then went over for the press conference.

Hundreds of thousands of journalists, so it seemed to me, had just been shown the film in a special press screening, and they were arrayed in a conference hall. The producers of the film and Miss Pidgeon and I were ushered into the conference hall and onto a stage. Many photographers took pictures, we were introduced by Henri Behar, the moderator and translator, and the press conference began.

People asked me questions, and I responded to them. People took pictures, the press conference ended, and we were ushered along by a nice burly Frenchman whom I took to be the director of security. We went through various passages of the Festival Hall, flanked by the burly man's myrmidons, who were all wearing madras jackets reminiscent of the fifties.

We ended up on a terrace at the side of the Festival

Hall. There were, arrayed on bleachers on the terrace, three hundred photographers popping off pictures. Flashbulbs kept going off, and people were screaming at me to look at them.

I would turn to look at them, and people from whom I had turned away would begin screaming that perhaps I should look back in their direction. This went on for the longest time. Twice I waved good-bye to the photographers and made as if to leave, and twice I was rebuffed by the festival officials, who indicated that they'd "be the judge of that."

Finally it was determined that all had gone correctly, and that the photographers on the bleachers were done.

My party was then directed to turn around, which we did, and found another hundred photographers on another terrace some fifty feet away, and then it was their turn and they took pictures for a while. Finally we were allowed to leave. A car drove us back to the Carlton, and I suggested to the driver that he have his wheels aligned, but he politely remonstrated that the offending oscillation was caused by myself, who was shaking like that which we in Vermont have come to know as "a leaf."

And I talked to some more journalists that afternoon, and then it was time to prepare for the big night.

Which of us has not confronted that tuxedo? Yes, our loved one is in the bathroom, engaged in god knows what procession of ritual preparations, and oblivious to all else. There is a spiritual apartheid between the bathroom and the bedroom. The usual connubial co-spiritedness that informs the happy home has ceased. One is alone.

I'd bought a new tuxedo, and was about to don it for the first time. The clothier suggested that I let out the waist a half-inch. I declined, as the waist fit right fine, I thought, and told him so. He suggested that as I was going to wear the tux with suspenders, rather than with a belt, I would be more comfy having the waist a bit looser. I knew, or thought I knew, that he was only being kind to me—and that, if I assented, he would let the waist an inch and a half and leave me, in my delusion, to believe he had let it out merely the promised half-inch—all of the above suspicions being justified by his use of slimming mirrors in his store.

So I told him not to let out the waist, and I started getting into the tux, and it fit *just fine* and rather loose around the waist, so I felt superior to my clothier, and then I thought that he had probably let the waist out *anyway,* and I suppressed an impulse to take the pants off and hunt for marks of the same.

Yes, my mind was racing.

I got into my tux by stages. There was a cunning little arrangement whereby the front of the stiff-front shirt was meant to attach itself through the inside of the fly of the pants, so as to keep the shirt nice 'n' neat and prevent its riding up. I finally got the arrangement to work, and then could not straighten up, so I redid it and got the bow tie tied and the whole nine yards and looked in the mirror and thought I looked pretty good.

Miss Pidgeon had bedecked herself in a stunning, very tight sequined dress and put on high-heeled shoes, and I lost my self-conscious vanity for a moment while I understood myself to be quite the luckiest man alive.

Down we went, we two fashion plates.

We went down into the lobby, and there were a load of paparazzi, and they took our picture.

One of the festival functionaries took us out the back

door, where it was still pissing down rain, and escorted us into one of the festival cars.

We made our way down the main drag at a footslogging pace. There were gendarmes with their cinematogenic kepis at the intersections, and there were two solid walls of folks from the hotel down to the Festival Hall, all along the blocked-off street. When we came abreast of the festival, the line of traffic halted completely. We stopped for several minutes at a time, and then inched forward a car length.

Ahead of us, at some unknown distance, cars were stopping to disgorge their precious cargo at the foot of the ceremonial red carpet of the Festival Hall.

We were in an overarching tunnel of people. They pressed up against the car, and the two sides seemed to reach over the top of the car and meet in the middle. People were popping flashbulbs and pounding on the car, and put their faces up against the windows.

They asked one another who it was in the car and, I must say, displayed rather good humor when they realized they did not recognize us.

We inched forward. The driver asked us to check to see if the rear doors were locked. This frightened me a bit.

I'd been to the Oscars twice, and thought them rather smashingly pagan, but this festival could give them Cards and Spades; the onlookers at the Oscars were just bored and vicious Americans like me, but *these* folks were interested in "film."

We arrived at our destination—the end of the red carpet. The doors were opened and we stood out under an insufficient canopy while it rained like a cow pissing on a flat rock, as they have it in Vermont.

We were held back from our ceremonial entrance as

various Continental celebrities went forward to the delight of the crowd. Then it came to be our turn. Up we went. Out from under the canopy and into the rain for fair. People took our pictures. I think the staircase was lined by double rows of someone or other.

I think that, after the fact, I was told there were trumpeters in Napoleonic livery, but I don't remember it.

I remember the gendarmes, who were all very young and very fit and stood quite still, with their hands clasped behind their back in parade rest, and they were very impressive. And I remember the troop of plainclothes bodyguards, who had changed their madras jackets to white-and-gray seersucker, and who looked very dap.

We went up the wide staircase of the Festival Hall (one of my film's producers likened the hall to the library of some midwestern university with a little too much money); up, I say, we went, and into the foyer and through that foyer into the vast auditorium. We were ushered to our seats.

On the stage, Geraldine Chaplin was speaking to the compere, a very relaxed and distinguished heavyset man in his sixties.

They called Roman Polanski up from the audience and introduced him as the chief judge of the festival this year, and he called the subordinate judges up, and they joined him on the stage.

I didn't know who many of them were, and my attention wandered. One of my film's producers introduced me to several of the Japanese backers of the movie, and we bowed and shook hands. Robert Mitchum was called out onstage, and he came flanked by two of his sons, and, in his quality of Prestigious Representative of World Cinema, he declared the festival open.

The compere asked for our, the audience's, forbearance, as the television equipment that had been obtruding on the stage was removed.

We, in the audience, chatted among ourselves for a while. Then the lights dimmed and the audience hushed.

We were shown a trailer for Polanski's *The Fearless Vampire Killers,* which was a nice historical touch; and then we were shown a trailer for *Citizen Kane,* which trailer starts and finishes with Orson Welles's trademark "Mercury Theatre of the Air" logo:

Limbo. A man's voice calls for a microphone. The mike swings in on a boom. A man's hand adjusts it, then retires from the shot. The voice (Welles) speaks, introducing the project we are about to see.

This trademark appears at the end of the Mercury films, too. Welles reiterates various facts, the casting of the film and other information, and the mike swings away and into limbo.

I've always thought that this trademark is one of the most classy things in the world. It fills me with both delight and envy each time I see it. I find myself not only impressed, but *regressed,* and the ultimate laurel of my youth escapes my open lips: "Cool."

Rest in peace, Mr. Welles, and I wish I had been privileged to know you.

And so we quieted down, and they showed my film.

My film was preceded by the "computer art" video logo of the festival. We see various free-floating steps, as if they are a staircase without the risers. We see that the steps are under water. The "camera" rises up the steps, and the steps emerge from the water and into the air. The steps keep rising through the air, and into the dark starry firmament. The top step tilts to the camera, and reveals, embossed, the palm-leaf colophon of the festival. This golden palm leaf takes leave of the step, which sinks away. It is then joined by various typography that tells us what we are looking at, and then it is over. I hate computers. I think they are the tool of the devil. In any case, they then showed my movie.

It was the first time I'd seen the film with a real audience.

I saw it for six months on the screen of a Steenbeck editing machine—this screen is about the size of a paperback book. During the editing process, I saw it a couple of times in a screening room with an audience of thirty or so handpicked folks.

Now here we are. The screen is 180 feet across, and there are twenty-five hundred folks like myself—jaded, blasé, anxious, and demanding—looking at my film.

Well, it did real good. Various people said various things about it afterward, but twenty-five hundred people paid attention for one hour and forty-two, and the film reflects my intentions as completely as I knew how to express them at that time, and it holds their attention, which indicates to me that, at least on a technical level, I did my job adequately well, and, beyond that, everything is with the gods.

Now, this whole issue of popular reception is a curious thing. I've been staging my work, plays and films, for twenty-some years. During that time I have striven to come to terms with the phenomena of popular and critical reception.

Popular reception is the easier to become comfortable with. I started out writing plays for my own theater company, and my relation to the audience was fairly clear—if one did one's job well, they paid attention, if not, then not. If it was funny, they laughed, if it was sad, they cried; if it was *not* funny, they did *not* laugh, and a person who persisted in the asseveration that his work was funny in opposition to the view of the audience might have a career in philosophy, but was not long for show business.

When the audience got *out* of the theater, another set of circumstances demanded recognition and understanding: the audience that perhaps *did* laugh and cry, might say, of the piece as a whole: "I didn't get it," or "I didn't like it."

In a theatrical environment, the audience signals this disaffection by staying away; if their presence at the play is paying your rent, you then starve.

So it is necessary to be very conscious of the audience, and work, I think, to help them understand your intention.

It is also necessary to learn to still the rancor that their lack of approval might create, and learn to evaluate this rancor and to respond to their opinion in one of two ways. One may respond to their disapproval either by saying (a) I see that I have not done my job sufficiently well—let me reexamine my work, and see if I could make it clearer; or (b) I, on reflection, think that my work is as clear as I can possibly make it, and I will resist the temptation to mutilate my work to please the audience.

If the work is paying the rent, one is, I think, fairly immune to the seductiveness of alternative (b), which goes under the name of Arrogance.

Dealing with critical reception is a bit more difficult—I think that critics are generally a bunch of unfortunates, and should be ashamed of themselves. Now, does this mean that I am philosophically immune to the desire for their praise? You may have already guessed the answer, which is no.

I have tried, over the years, to wean myself from this desire. I have repeated, fervently and oft, the wise words of Epictetus, who said: "Do you seek the good opinion of these people? Are they not the same people who, you told me yesterday, are frauds and imbeciles? Do you then seek the good opinion of frauds and imbeciles?"

Well, I guess I do. I'm trying not to.

For a few years I didn't read reviews.

Most of us in the hurly-burly world of the stage tell one another that we don't read reviews, and we all pretend to believe one another. But, for whatever it's worth, for a couple of years I didn't read reviews, and was a much better man for it.

Now the reductio ad absurdum of the artist-critic *combat* is the juried competition.

It contains the worst elements of critical autocracy and committee compromise.

What *can* it mean that one film or actor or play is better than all the rest, and that we may rest assured of its distinction because of the imprimatur of a "group of folks"? What can that mean? Well, it doesn't mean *anything*. Unless, of course, you win.

And that's why I had fallen off the ladder and brought my film to Cannes, and that's why I was sitting there, whore that I am, watching my movie with twenty-five hundred people dressed in what used to be called "formal wear."

The film ended, and they hit the general area of my seat with lights, and the audience applauded. (One reviewer, whose work I am aware of through having read it, said that the audience gave the film a standing ovation. My memory runs to the contrary, but . . .)

I stood up and wondered whether to ask Miss Pidgeon

to take a bow with me. I sat back down, the audience applauded some more, and I stood up again, all the time wondering if I should ask her to stand with me. I was of two minds about it. I sat down again. They turned the lights off. I should have asked her to stand with me. My party was ushered out of the main hall and into the foyer. There we were placed in a human square formed by gendarmes. These gendarmes, about fifteen on a side, stood with their backs to us and kept us separated from a group, the audience, who had no interest in us whatsoever.

The plainclothes bodyguards, who had changed their jackets again, and now sported very nice reddish plaid affairs, escorted us out some side way of the festival and down to the harborside, where a huge tent had been erected.

We walked under various marquees, whipped by rain. The marquees were near to blowing away, and it was cold.

We went down into the tent, where there appeared to be seating for seven or eight hundred.

We were shown our table, and sat down. I had vowed, for reasons of general health, not to drink anything during the trip, but conceived an existential desire to nullify that vow, and I asked anyone who would listen if they knew where I could get a stiff double shot of something. Everyone said I was out of luck, but waiters started bringing wine to the table, and I started drinking it.

Jack Lang, the cultural minister of France, was seated down the table. My producer had given me a commemorative trinket from our movie, to present to him, but I never got around to it. Robert Mitchum was also at the table, and I went over and said how pleased I was to meet him, and he nodded.

I was seated between Miss Pidgeon and my good friend and agent, Howard.

Down at our end of the table were also a French movie star and his friend, who was a director of opera. This movie star was very taken with the film, and talked about it at length, and made me feel very good.

We sat around talking and drinking wine. The waiters brought the food, which was very French, and magnificent, and piping hot, which last was, I thought, quite a feat for a meal for eight hundred people in a tent in the rain.

Men I took to be producers began roaming from table to table and standing in the narrow and impossibly crowded aisles. Many of these men smoked cigars.

An African singer was introduced, and went up on the stage and played some very beautiful music on a native stringed instrument, and sang in accompaniment.

The atmosphere either became or appeared very smoky, and I felt a certain, dare I say, orgiastic undertone growing in the tent. We Levitical priests had performed our ceremony and retired into the tabernacle, which for the unanointed to approach was death, and we had taken our girdles off.

What strange, what wild and unforeseeable revelry would ensue as the evening continued its inevitable progress toward the dawn? With which of the young starlets would the producers retire?

What magnificent diversion, fresh from the opium dens of Indo-Chine, would the sophisticates elect and practice?

Would they gash one another's flesh and drink one another's blood?

Would they play liar's poker for the souls of the yet unborn? Would they hug and kiss . . . ?

Well, I can't tell you, 'cause I'm not much of a party-goer, and I and Miss Pidgeon went home.

We said good-bye to the movie star and the opera director, who were a lovely pair of people, and quite a welcome bit of friendship and show-business hospitality, and we went out into the rain, which I have described before, and the wind, which I shall limn as an "enraged monster, whipping now this way and now that."

The bodyguards—I know you will not believe me—had changed their jackets once again and now sported white piqué affairs, and they helped us down the line of now-deserted marquees, and into a car, which took us back to the hotel.

Miss Pidgeon and I got into our bathrobes, and sat around dissecting the evening's events.

The phone rang. It was our friend Brigitte. She was down in the lobby, and had been missing us at each stage of the evening's festivities. We invited her up. She said that she was in the company of several members of our film's production-distribution team. We invited them up, too. Up they came.

There was a rather splendid bottle of champagne in the room, sent by an agent friend, with a well-wishing note that concluded: "Today Cannes, Tomorrow the World, then the Creative Artists Agency."

Brigitte and the crew previously described sat on the floor, and the men loosened their bow ties and took off their jackets and smoked cigars. We drank the champagne, and emptied the minibar, and Brigitte took pictures of Miss Pidgeon and myself sitting on our bed in our bathrobes.

The next morning, Friday, Miss Pidgeon and I awoke. The room smelled of cigar smoke.

We decided to enshrine the events of the last wee hours in our collective memory as "the night of the penguins." We went down for coffee.

That Friday noon found us at the Hôtel du Cap, in the space that, the producer told me, had been Nazi headquarters for southern France.

We had our lunch, and talked in an open and friendly fashion with many journalists, most of whom would probably, thinking of their responsibility to their readership, turn around and cut us to shreds; but it was a lovely lunch.

That afternoon was spent chatting with various groups of international press, and I don't remember what we did that evening.

The next day was warm and clear, a beautiful day to sit out on the beach, looking at the harbor. But our plans were otherwise.

Brigitte was taking Miss Pidgeon's picture, and I had a couple of hours to kill. I walked down the Croisette, by the Festival Hall, which area was now, of course, deserted.

Down by the city hall I found a flea market, and I was in heaven for a half hour or so.

I bought a pot-metal barrette depicting a rooster, to bring back for my assistant, Harriet.

I bought a beautiful ceramic water jug in the shape of a crow, and bearing the legend HÔTEL DU CORBEAU.

I walked back to the hotel and bought commemorative T-shirts and trinkets for children and friends.

The concessionaire was a very old and very polite man. He took a great deal of time with me, opening each plastic-wrapped T-shirt to display the difference between the French idea of medium and their idea of large. He offered me several mints, and I took them. At the conclusion of the transaction a middle-aged woman, to whom this man deferred, entered the shop with her French poodle and walked behind the counter. This woman paid scant attention to the old man, who reiterated the details of our transaction. He showed the woman my bill, which he was in the process of preparing.

She acknowledged him hardly at all, and told me the total price, and I paid her and took my souvenirs. On my way out of the store, the man gave me another small packet of mints, and I thanked him.

Miss Pidgeon and I drove back to the airport in Nice.

THE BUTTONS ON
THE BOARD

First, I should like to speak of the Topperweins.

Ad and his wife, Plinky Topperwein, were trick-shot artists. They played vaudeville, and toured also for the Winchester Repeating Arms Company, whose products they used and promoted.

I was once at an auction in New York to benefit the arms-and-armor collection of the Metropolitan Museum of Art. Among the many beautiful and belligerophiliant items put up for sale there was the trunk of the Topperweins.

It contained many of their playbills and posters; it contained several of their hats and other articles of clothing; it contained two model-63 Winchester .22 pump rifles, one of which was guaranteed to be one of the battery with which Ad shot forty-three thousand two-inch wooden cubes out of the air. It contained, as if all this were insufficient, several of the copper "rifle portraits" that Plinky and Ad shot as part of their various demonstrations.

These portraits were two-by-three-foot thin copper

sheets that, in the demonstration, were put at a distance from the shooter, and on which he or she inscribed, by means of the .22 Long Rifle cartridge, a portrait of (to choose from their repertoire) George Washington, an Indian chief, a turkey, Abraham Lincoln, and so on.

I had heard much of these copper sheets, but, prior to the auction, the only one I had ever seen was in the shop of a celebrated gunsmith in Louisiana, which portrait was definitely not for sale.

So I sat amazed as, one after another, beautiful Edwardian artifacts came out of the trunk; mementos of shooting, and show business, and, in short, the dream material of "another time"; and, for some reason I couldn't tell you, I did not bid on the trunk.

I think I was one of the only people in the audience who knew of the Topperweins (my knowledge coming more from the show business than from the shooting side of my experience), so the bidding did not go very high. The trunk went cheap, and somebody else bought it.

What would it have meant, I ask myself—as, perhaps, many of you who are collectors of this and that do; what would it have meant to have possessed that trunk, that trinket, that connection to another time, or that suggestion to ourselves or others of another aspect of ourselves; what would it mean, and why is the longing for the unobtainable worse than the transmutation of the unobtainable into the everyday? (For, my reluctance to bid on the trunk was, finally, a refusal to contribute to the transmutation.)

In any case, some years later I saw, in a tray at an antiques show, a pin-back button, one inch across, promoting the Topperweins, and I bought it. The button bears a photograph of the two. She is a bluff and bulky-looking individual in a white shirt and black tie. She has a large mouth and dark hair. He is standing next to her in a dark suit. He has a thick mustache, and looks to be the passive one of the pair. Both wear large-brimmed hats, his blocked in the "trooper" fashion.

The button reads THE WONDERFUL TOPPERWEINS. WHO ALWAYS SHOOT WINCHESTER GUNS AND CARTRIDGES.

Inside the button's back is the maker's mark: WHITE-HEAD AND HOAG COMPANY (BUTTONS, BADGES, NOVELTIES, AND SIGNS), NEWARK, NEW JERSEY.

Whitehead and Hoag invented and patented the pin-back button in the 1890s. This mode of advertisement caught on immediately, and was soon used to promote any and everything thought remotely promotable. Politicians, comic strips, newspaper give-aways, religion, temperance, fraternal associations, and every article of merchandise and every service of that period can be found advertised on pin-back buttons.

Over the years I have collected, displayed, traded, and hoarded buttons. I have worn them and given them away as jewelry; I have even commissioned some.

Since I became attracted to the form, I have always stuck them in the wall or molding or bulletin board near any writing desk that I was using over any extended period.

Now, the above sentence displays a strained circumlocution for and reveals an inability to employ the term *office*. It is, perhaps, that inability or refusal to face the indignity of self-knowledge which has led me, over the years, to adorn my workplace with what, to me, are the artifacts of romance.

I do not want to be at the desk. I want to be at a place and in a time alluded to by these mementos. And, further than a *creed*, my *assertion*, while in my office at my desk, is "anywhere but here."

The buttons are not mere reminders, they are survivors, the archeological artifacts of the dream kingdom where, if and when I am doing my job effectively, I spend what I suppose must be called my working hours.

Stuck in the corkboard, directly in front of me as I write, is a six-point metal star that looks to be nickel over iron or steel. It is embossed APACHE POLICE, SAN CARLOS, ARIZ., and has a small brass head of an American Indian in feather headdress brazed into its center. The badge seems to have seen a lot of wear and use. Directly to the right is a small cloisonné pin in blue, with a large white cross in the center. Sailing out of the cross is a black-and-red ocean liner, and below, in gold, is written AMERICAN RELIEF SHIP FOR SPAIN. To the right again is a half-inch-diameter celluloid button with a girl's face on it.

The button's back informs us that it was, again, made by the Whitehead and Hoag Company, and that they, in this case, are advertising Perfection cigarettes. This girl's picture, it seems, was one of a series depicting types of feminine beauty that one could obtain and examine at leisure through the purchase of the Perfection brand.

The girl on the button is dark honey-blond, with correspondingly blue eyes, rosy cheeks, a bee-stung mouth, and a mole on the left side of her lip. She is placid and rather expressionless, I think; and her face is full and somewhat heavy, and childlike, and very much in line with the fin-de-siècle American notion of beauty. Perfect, heavy, regular, and docile—the picture would not, today, be recognizable as an attempt to depict feminine allurements.

154

And we would find the picture on the adjacent button odd by contemporary standards. It shows a happy Boy Scout in his campaign hat and red neckerchief. His white face beams boldly out from the blue background, smiling a wide, delighted, and unreserved smile. A linen ribbon is affixed to the button's back and reads CAMPOREE—1935.

And, next to him is a rare employee's badge from the 1933 World's Fair, the Chicago Century of Progress Exposition, which may give a clue to the boy's expression.

That World's Fair was the most recent celebration of the final subjugation of the material world. It was the apotheosis of the notion of technology as grace. The innocent, happy, and overall *hopeful* Boy Scout was blessed to live on the very verge of that time for which his forefathers had striven: the future.

The deliberate, laudable, and serious rectitude of the Victorian Age had vanished in the unaccountable appearance of the First World War and the madness of the twenties, but society was once again on track and all of a mind; and the noble though outmoded notion of duty had been supplanted by the more perfect ideal of progress.

For what was that girl going to do, but court and marry, and give birth to and raise children? And why should she not be placid—for, if introspection and anxiety and anger were a part (as, of course they were) of her life, they were not a part of her age's ideal of beauty, as they are in our age.

To the left of the Apache police star is a metal-plant identification badge. It is stamped EBALOY. ROCKFORD, IL. FOUNDARIES INC. And numbered 708. It is a sandwich: two layers of metal, between which the employee's photo was to have been put, so as to be visible through a window in the badge's front. The photo it carries now is not of the original employee; it is a snapshot cut out of a proof sheet of 35-mm black-and-white film.

Even on the proof sheet, the photographic quality is extraordinarily good. We see a man and woman with their arms around each other, smiling at the camera. They both have on short leather jackets and sunglasses and baseball caps. They are standing on what seems to be a wharf or a pier. Behind them we see the water of a harbor, and a small fishing boat tied up to a pier opposite.

We can see that the woman is very beautiful. She has long dark hair, a lovely smile. She is very slender and graceful.

Sometime, eventually, this button will be destroyed. Sometime, it is likely, before it vanishes, someone will look at it and wonder who the man and woman could have been; and perhaps that person will make up stories about them. For, there they are, very little different from the Topperweins, woman on the left, man on the right, a head taller; two couples smiling at the camera, and what can they have been thinking that day, and who were they?

A foot or so off to the right on the bulletin board is Dwight Eisenhower's picture on a cheap piece of tin. It says I LIKE IKE, and has the five stars of his army rank below the photograph.

And there's the union button I picked out of the gutter—a crimson rectangle that reads, STANDING WITH THE UNION. I SUPPORT THE HARVARD UNION OF CLERICAL AND TECHNICAL WORKERS. And I remember finding it. It was a rainy day in Cambridge, Massachusetts. And there had been quite a bit of agitation and, I think, bad feeling—on both sides of an issue that had to do, I believe, with the right of Harvard employees to organize, or to strike, or to do something that they, as a group, desired and another group opposed.

In any case, when I saw it I thought the STANDING WITH THE UNION button rather unusual, as it was a rectangle, standing the long-way up. I thought it rather clunky and unbeautiful. But I looked down at it, in the rain, in the gutter, and I thought that I would add it to my collection. But no, I thought, you didn't appreciate the button when you saw it displayed legitimately on the clothing of the antagonists, how could you be so greedy as to covet it now, in the gutter? I castigated myself with the accusation of having a taste for trash, rather than a clean and legitimate nostalgia. So I walked on down the street for a while, and then I turned around and came back and picked up the button.

For it had not been sufficiently removed from me to endow it with any of the totemic power of a romantic article, and to enshrine it *myself,* without the intervening purification of a mercantile transaction, felt like a Gnostic leap of faith, and it made me uncomfortable.

But, nonetheless, I took it back, and stuck it in the bulletin board in my office, off to one side. And as the months and then the year or so passed since its acquisition—as I removed buttons from the board to wear them, or to give them away, or just to change the design, I moved the Harvard button into a more and more prominent position; and comforted myself with the twin notions that it was being cleansed by time, and that someday, with my dissolution, it would be completely purified.

157

ABOUT THE AUTHOR

DAVID MAMET is the author of various plays, including *American Buffalo, Speed-the-Plow, Glengarry Glen Ross* (for which he won the Pulitzer Prize), and *Oleanna*, and the screenplays for *The Verdict, The Untouchables, Hoffa,* and others. He has directed the films *Homicide, House of Games,* and *Things Change* (written with Shel Silverstein). He lives in Massachusetts and Vermont.